A Guide to Abney Park Cemetery

1 Monument to
Isaac Watts DD

A GUIDE TO ABNEY PARK CEMETERY

PAUL JOYCE

AN ABNEY PARK CEMETERY TRUST PUBLICATION

Patron Baroness Blackstone of Stoke Newington
Registered Charity No 1005334   Company No 2634036
Registered address: 109 Winston Road Stoke Newington London N16 9LN

SECOND EDITION
1994

2 Monument to Walter Milburn Ball among obelisks in Road I.

Contents

Foreword

It comes as something of a shock, as all cemeteries do. Driving through the traffic up Stamford Hill, the eye is inevitably caught by those daunting Egyptian pylons at the gates. An even more telling intimation of mortality comes in Church Street, where those lovely wrought-iron gates were made to open upon lawns, flower-beds and a comfortable house but, at second glance, now lead to nowhere but the grave.

Such melancholy may be the introduction to Abney Park Cemetery – and it is a gentle, unfrightening melancholy – but thereafter all is as pleasant as one trusts it is, for its present inmates, in the hereafter. For a start, these are green acres and London, or Hackney, to be precise, or Stoke Newington to be exact, can do with all the greenery it can get. Here must be as many varieties of wild birds as can be found within many miles of Charing Cross, together with the wild flowers and shrubs and the trees that attract them, giving another meaning to Mr James Branwhite French's words in his *Walks in Abney Park* of 1883, 'Death is but a contrivance for gaining more life.' For here the diligent may find such as sow thistle, red campion, nipplewort and Japanese knotweed growing amongst English oaks and chestnuts and foreign Indian bean tree and swamp cypress. Look amongst them for mistle thrush and carrion crow, spotted flycatcher and great spotted woodpecker.

This, too, is an architectural theme park, illustrated by Victorian architects, sculptors and monumental masons. Here can be found the meaning of mysterious words like acroteria, apsidal and baldaquin.

There is another, more subtle, aspect of Abney Park; one that would have appealed particularly to Victorian sensibilities. Its paths are for strolling and musing as well as bird-watching and architectural study. And what better to muse upon than questions of life and death, or to be specific, the lives and deaths of those who built this place and those for whom it was built? Here you can meet, as much as is permitted by the laws of mortality, such as General William Booth of the Salvation Army; Frank Bostock, the zoo-keeper; Josiah Conder, the bookseller; Agnes Forsyth, the three-year-old daughter of the sculptor James Forsyth; the Hibberds, the editor of gardening magazines, and his wife; many more North London worthies crowd beneath the trees. In a wildly fanciful moment, one could imagine a Stanley Spencer resurrection-day as a mid-Victorian garden-party.

3 Funeral Cortège of General William Booth arriving at Abney Park Cemetery on 29 August 1912, from a photograph by the Cyclorama Photocrom Company.

None of this – the sylvan glades, the wildlife park, the exhibition of nineteenth century taste in monuments, the setting for philosophical meditation – would be available but for the Save Abney Park Cemetery movement and the sympathetic support of Hackney Borough Council. Now Paul Joyce, assisted by Alan Hunt, has written a guide to this delightfully haunted place, opening our eyes to its hidden treasures and giving our appreciation of London a new dimension that combines the past with the present.

Tom Pocock

Acknowledgements

The publication of this book, a joint initiative of the Save Abney Park Cemetery association and the Planning Division of the London Borough of Hackney, has been made possible by grants through the Inner City Partnership Programme, although it should be stated that the opinions expressed herein are the responsibility of SAPC and the author and do not necessarily reflect the views of the Council.

Personal thanks are due to Ashley Godfrey and Mike New of the Planning Division, and to Peter Salter of Save Abney Park Cemetery for their consistent interest and encouragement in the production of the text; also to Alan Hunt of SAPC and the Royal Society for the Protection of Birds for his important contribution of a chapter on the cemetery's natural life.

Full advantage has been taken of the research facilities and ever courteous assistance provided by the Local History Librarians of Stoke Newington and Hackney, and especially Miss J Dailey with her encyclopaedic knowledge of Stoke Newington sources both recondite and familiar; also the late Stanley Tongue, and Jean Wait of Hackney Borough Archives, and of the generous permission to reproduce material in their charge. Dr Brent Elliott, Librarian of the Royal Horticultural Society; the Guildhall Librarians of the City of London; and Keepers of the Greater London Council Records, have all given me access to valuable information.

Neither could I have done without the kindly co-operation of David Ruddiman and his staff at Abney Park Cemetery; here the resourceful aid of George Bailey pointed me towards several hitherto fugitive monuments. Facts too numerous to list have been gleaned from local inhabitants, as well as from Nemone Lethbridge and members of SAPC; advice and support from Dr Michael Hunter and other members both of the Hackney Society and the Victorian Society.

Alan Tucker undertook sundry photographic tasks including a number of illustrations taken specially for this book; Ian Wallace drew the reference plan; Laura Thomas patiently contended with my much gone over pages of manuscript and transformed them into a faultless typescript; Margery Craig and several of the above-mentioned volunteered to read and criticise the eventual result. For all these improving influences I am extremely grateful.

Finally, a very particular indebtedness must be recorded: to Tom Pocock of the London Evening Standard for his Foreword and, moreover, for his splendid gift to SAPC, and so ultimately to the Borough of Hackney, of the original wrought iron over-throw from the Abney House Gate in Church Street, which he had astutely salvaged and restored when the cemetery's fortunes seemed at their lowest ebb.

Paul Joyce   Stoke Newington   1983

Preface

At a time when the comparatively new subject of cemetery studies is appearing on the curriculum of many universities and polytechnics, there is a particular value in placing on record one of the most fascinating and attractive Victorian cemeteries in England. Too long ignored, it is an essential part of our heritage, impossible to replace, difficult to forget.

Hackney's act in rescuing Abney Park Cemetery from unmistakeable, and unimaginable, ruin in 1979 was urged on by the local conservationists. It was clearly the only possible move. But what could best be put forward as the future role of this beautifully wooded and still partly wild place? Its obvious qualities as a nature reserve and a secluded haven for people to briefly retreat into depend on careful maintenance and a long term strategy of cleaning up, replanting, and many other environmental improvements.

Although these are ideas as yet at the discussion stage, it is intended that a comprehensive and sensitive plan will soon emerge. Meanwhile, urgent structural works have gone ahead, and the partnership between the Borough Council and the local Voluntary Association has undoubtedly been one of Hackney's recent success stories. It includes among other things the reinstatement of railings, gates and lodges, landscaping the entrance forecourt, and reroofing the chapel, besides making possible the restoration of the monument to Isaac Watts, Abney Park's resident patron saint.

Because its time as a burial ground is now strictly limited, safeguarding the cemetery as an enjoyable public asset falls into line with revised, and more sophisticated, attitudes to historic buildings and sites. Instead of neglect and destruction, we are now moved to retain and prize what has somehow managed to survive. Abney Park has, after all, its own unique history steeped in the deep-rooted traditions of English political and religious dissent, as the timely appearance of this book – exactly one hundred years after the last guide to the cemetery – sets out to relate.

I hope that after reading it, those who might otherwise pass by the serene gates with detachment will come to explore and appreciate the rich diversity of interest within.

Richard Gee   1983
Chairman   Planning and Transport Committee
London Borough of Hackney

Preface to the second edition

Since the original publication of this guide ten years ago, the management of Abney Park Cemetery has passed from the London Borough of Hackney into the hands of the Abney Park Cemetery Trust.

The Trust was inaugurated on 20 May 1992, one hundred and fifty two years to the day after the ceremonial opening of Abney Park Cemetery in 1840. The signing of the 21-year lease underlined the Trust's intention to maintain the cemetery as an historic landscape and managed wilderness, available to all for the pursuit of education, leisure and remembrance. To this end, the South Lodge had been converted into an information centre. Then in June 1993 the cemetery was designated a Local Nature Reserve in recognition of its abundance of wild flowers, fungi, mature trees and wildlife – all these the more precious for being at the centre of a busy urban area. More recently still, the restoration of the main gates and forecourt has helped return the public face of the cemetery to its former dignity. Future plans include the rehabilitation of the chapel and the replanting of the arboretum.

Paul Joyce's book has been described as the finest guide to a Victorian cemetery yet published and, into the bargain, contains an excellent history of Stoke Newington. It is in recognition of this, and also to mark its ambition to promote due appreciation of a major local asset, that the Trust has decided to publish a second edition.

The driving force behind the first edition in the early eighties was the Save Abney Park Cemetery association. This later evolved into the Friends of Abney Park Cemetery, who then went on to form the Abney Park Cemetery Trust. Many of those earlier enthusiasts are still involved with the cemetery and the Trust wishes to record its appreciation of their many years of good work. It also wishes to thank the London Borough of Hackney, and in particular Councillor Tommy Sheppard, for their pivotal support in the Trust's formation. The Council continues to meet the Trust's core costs and provides assistance in gaining funding.

Finally, the Trust would like to thank Paul Joyce for his co-operation in preparing this second edition, and for the enormous contribution he has made towards the cemetery's welfare over past years.

Nemone Lethbridge

Nemone Lethbridge   1993
Abney Park Cemetery Trust
The South Lodge   Abney Park Cemetery
Stoke Newington High Street
London   N16 0AS

Note to the second edition

For the sake of history and economy, it has been decided to reissue this guide in its original form. But inevitably, since its first publication a decade ago, much in Abney Park Cemetery has changed. So too has some of our knowledge of its past. To accommodate this, many small amendments have been made to the text. Less absorbable in this way is the rediscovery of several important graves – those of William Adolphus Knell (1801-1875) the Victorian marine painter, Path Q N/C3, and Emily Goss (1806-1857) the naturalist, Little Elm Walk E/C6, being the most eminent, although James De Foe (1778-1857) great grandson of Daniel Defoe, Path O S/F3, also deserves mention.

The SAPC Survey of Monuments, commenced 1980, culminated in the publication of the guide in 1984. This was closely followed by SAPC's Restoration of Monuments programme. Carried out in four stages during 1986-91, it resulted in the reconstruction, repair or cleaning of no less than 125 monuments and tombs, clearance of undergrowth being done in conjunction with the masons' work. The impact on the landscape was startling, but nowhere more so than at Abney House Corner whose unsightly piles of bomb-damaged stones were sorted out and re-erected in their rightful places. At the same time, Dr Nathaniel Rogers' splendid mausoleum was cleaned – it at length received its new ironwork gate and grille in 1992.

There have been upsets too. The theft of the whistful portrait medallion of Horace Kimbell was surely the most distressing; it is now replaced by a copy. Agnes Forsyth's and John Spreat's monuments were both practically demolished, the former by vandals, the latter by a storm, but they were able to be recon-structed without obvious harm. As to the chapel, slates continue to disappear from its rebuilt roof, although on the positive side, foundations and structure were stabilised in 1987-88.

Always something of a compromise, with its municipal shrub beds and concrete bollards, the 1980s layout of the entrance forecourt has been superseded by a more correctly historical approach. Yorkstone paving and granite setts are retained, but the new ironwork barrier rail is an exact copy of that which formerly existed. This excellent work was carried out by the Trust in 1993.

Since this book was written, the local history collections of Hackney and Stoke Newington have become absorbed into the central LBH Archives, where cited documents must now be sought.

It remains for me to express my thanks to Greg McNeill of the Abney Park Cemetery Trust for his enthusiastic encouragement in the making of this new edition.

Paul R Joyce

Paul Joyce   Upper Clapton   1993

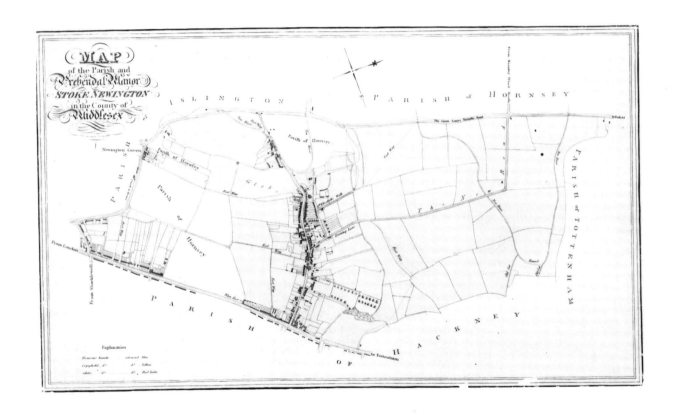

The Abney Estate
an historical introduction

4 Map of the Manor of Stoke Newington based on a survey of 1814 by William Merrington, engraved by R Bowler in 1820 for William Robinson's History of Stoke Newington. The township is concentrated around Church Street (centre) between the High Road (bottom left) and Green Lanes (top). Hackney Brook divides the parish into two roughly equal parts northward of Church Street, and further north the New River loops across the meadows round Woodberry Down. Here the New Road is an extension of Lordship Road. The outlines of the Abney and Fleetwood estates are visible north of the High Road end of Church Street, with the elm walks and long orchard prominently marked out. Ten Acre Field on Stamford Hill is at the lowest, most eastern point of the map.

Although Abney Park has existed in its present form only since 1827 when the previously fragmented sections of two distinct old estates were assembled under a single proprietor, it retains both by its title and by its associations intimate historical links with the Manor of Stoke Newington through the heyday of puritanism and beyond, traceable in some detail to the acquisition of these properties by the families of Hartopp and Gunston during the course of the seventeenth century. By the marriage of Lieutenant General Charles Fleetwood into the Hartopp household and subsequently of Sir Thomas Abney into Gunston's the two great mansions, side by side on the north of Church Street, were to receive their familiar and enduring names.

The magnificently arboured grounds attached to these mansions formed in earlier times part of an extensive sweep of broad meadowlands rising imperceptibly northward from the small township to a belt of scattered woodlands crowning the slopes of Woodberry Down. They were bounded on the south-east by a section of the great Roman highway from London to Lincoln known as Ermine Street (here represented by High Street and Stamford Hill), and on their western flank by the Green Lanes of perhaps equal antiquity. Through the northern parts of this open meadowland the New River, created in 1608-13, described a generous loop before its downward course through Newington to Clerkenwell; further southward the Hackney Brook cut circuitously through the meadows to delve under Stamford Bridge on its irregular eastward route via Hackney to the River Lea. All these lands **4** within the ancient parish boundaries were held either in lease or in copyhold tenure from the Lords of the Manor, but any consideration of the manor before the mid-nineteenth century is compounded by the circumstances of its actual ownership, for near on one thousand years, by the Cathedral of St Paul in London.

Until well after the Reformation there is no account of its direct administration, although the manor was in all probability leased out by the successive Prebendaries of Newington in St Paul's by long-standing tradition. Changes brought in at the commencement of Elizabeth's reign deprived the last Catholic Prebendary under Mary Tudor's regime of all rank, replacing him in 1559 by Thomas Penny. On becoming the earliest certain Protestant Prebendary of Newington, Penny appears to have lost no time in leasing out the entire properties to William Patten, the first non-clerical Lord of the Manor of whom record survives. This situation of manor lessees persisted in Stoke Newington until the Church land reforms of the nineteenth century and certainly had some beneficial effects on the place despite the cumbersome legalities it brought to bear on subsequent allocations of lands. As a man of substance, Teller of the Receipt of the Queen's Exchequer at Westminster and a JP for Middlesex, Patten took a kindly interest in the affairs of the township, providing means for an almost complete rebuilding of the then near-ruinous church of St Mary in 1563. Of this date the tower and south aisle, built in red

21 brick, are still basically intact in the existing fabric picturesquely enfolded in the verges of Clissold Park. Nearby to the east of the churchyard, its site now taken by the Municipal Offices and Library, stood the old Manor House with pleasure grounds extending northward to the eastern limb of the present park where Queen Elizabeth's Walk, once the elm-lined promenade leading out of these grounds across the Home Field to Hackney Brook, owes its name by tradition of the great Queen's visit to the Earl of Leicester during his probable temporary residence in the 1580's.

Whether William Patten ever lived there is doubtful but he did not in any case remain long, having disposed of the leasehold by 1571 to John Dudley, then already in occupation for at least two years. Although Dudley himself died in 1580 he generated through his daughter Anne a dynasty of lessee Lords of the Manor which flourished up to the close of the seventeenth century, so that his elaborate monument of coloured alabaster with kneeling figures and high-flown Latin inscription is justifiably the chief ornament of the Old Parish Church. His widow married again in c1582. Her second husband, the distinguished civil servant turned merchant Thomas Sutton, posthumously celebrated as founder of Charterhouse Hospital in Clerkenwell, thus came by interests in the manor until his wife's death in 1602, but the 15-year-old Anne Dudley had meanwhile, in 1590, become the wife of Sir Francis Popham and in the following year the lease was assigned to them. The Pophams and their descendants were to be associated with Stoke Newington throughout the upheavals of the seventeenth century. Sir Francis, subsequently one of the most zealous of the Parliamentarians, died in 1644 a sworn opponent of King Charles I; during the first Civil War, his second son and heir Alexander rose to the rank of Colonel in the Parliamentary Army and was thereafter elevated to Cromwell's House of Lords. On the sequestration of Church lands by Parliament in 1649 Alexander Popham accordingly purchased the prebendal estate of Newington and proceeded to install himself, for the brief duration of the

5 Fleetwood House, the entrance front, drawn by T H Shepherd in 1843.

Commonwealth, first and last Lord of the Manor by virtue of freehold owner-ship. Eventually, following the Restoration, when the Church recovered its looted properties he was obliged to surrender his gains but having made his peace with King Charles II, resumed his former role as lessee. Colonel Popham and his successors let out the fast-dilapidating Manor House at Stoke Newington, preferring instead to live in relative obscurity at their country estate in Wiltshire. Apart from the Pophams the most prominent family to become established in the parish before the Commonwealth was that of Hartopp, in process of building a town house here during the early 1630s.

It appears likely that Sir Edward Hartopp, the first Baronet, had purchased the copyhold of several acres of land on the north of Church Street soon after 1628 when he first sat in Parliament for his native Leicestershire and therefore required an occasional residence within easy reach of Westminster. In spite of the scanty evidence relating to the origins of this estate, it is reasonably clear that the first Baronet and his son Sir Edward were both then involved in building the spacious red brick mansion later to be known as Fleetwood **5** House, also that it had been completed by 1635. It stood in a large garden and shrubbery with extensive frontage to Church Street, the whole of which is

now occupied by the fire station together with the properties between Fleetwood Street and Summerhouse Road. Further back beyond the garden and shrubbery lay eight acres of grounds bounded on the north by Hackney Brook, a narrower strip extending eastward alongside the brook until it reached the High Street by Stamford Bridge. The later history of Fleetwood House is of such intricacy owing to its substantial enlargement at the end of the seventeenth century when further land was obtained, and its radical external transformation a half-century afterwards when it had become permanently divided into two separate residences, that it is now quite impossible to form any but the most approximate impression of its original
6 state or style. However, that it was an exceedingly ambitious piece of house-building there can be no question; big casement windows, some containing coats of arms in stained glass, lit its many rooms superbly panelled in wainscot; the staircases were massive in highly wrought timberwork, and one of the great apartments boasted a rich plasterwork ceiling ornamented with armorial devices demonstrating the Hartopp pedigree. Here also on this ceiling duly appeared the arms of Coke of Melbourne when in 1634 the younger Sir Edward Hartopp married Mary, daughter of Sir John Coke. It seems a bizarre irony that Sir Edward, cousin to the Catholic poet John Dryden

6 Fleetwood House, a view of the garden front, from a photograph taken shortly before its demolition in 1872.

whose own family espoused the Parliamentarian cause, had been knighted in the year of his marriage by King Charles I at the romantic, but ill-fated, Castle of Belvoir; when the Civil War broke out he threw in his lot with Parliament against the King and raised a regiment for Cromwell, although his reputation as a soldier is not very considerable. Having succeeded to the baronetcy in 1654 he did not long enjoy it, dying at the age of 50 in 1658. The house at Stoke Newington then fell to his widow Dame Mary Hartopp, their 20-year-old son Sir John Hartopp, third Baronet (1637-1722), and their daughter Mary. These three represented a family prominent in the affairs of religious dissent in the decades following the Restoration, and were soon to be fortified by alignment with a yet more elevated dissenter in the person of Charles Fleetwood of Feltwell (1618-1692).

After training for a legal career at Gray's Inn, Fleetwood entered the civil strife in 1642 and rose to Colonel in two years, gathering notoriety on the way as a favourer of preaching officers. To his credit he took no part in the second Civil War, nor in the King's trial and execution, and so escaped the calumny and degradation of the regicides on the accession of Charles II. Nonetheless his loyalty to the Independents' cause justified the great confidence placed in him by Oliver Cromwell who, by promoting him to Lieutenant General in 1650, cleared the way for his leading part in the Battle of Worcester in September 1651. A few weeks after this event Fleetwood's wife Frances Smith died leaving him with two young children to rear; within days of her funeral a similar calamity overtook Cromwell's amanuensis General Henry Ireton. Ireton's widow Bridget, the Protector's eldest daughter, became Charles Fleetwood's second wife in 1652 thus placing him at a stroke at the centre of power in the Commonwealth. By taking Ireton's place in Cromwell's affections he superseded him first as Commander-in-Chief, then from 1654 as Lord Deputy in Ireland, a position handed over to his brother-in-law Henry in 1657. Recalled to England in 1655 he assumed a leading role in the Lord Protector's court and there is some probability that his father-in-law made provision for Fleetwood's succession, not only to full command of the army but as head of the Commonwealth. Oliver's death in September 1658 left all question of a successor in disarray but although search was made for documents in which the Lieutenant General was thought to be named, none ever came to light, due perhaps to their prompt disposal by one of the Protector's daughters. Notwithstanding this curious contretemps, Fleetwood engaged in the elevation of Richard Cromwell to the protectorate, receiving in turn highest preferment as Commander-in-Chief during the confusions of 1659.

Recorded opinions of Fleetwood's character have varied considerably, but that he was both a distinguished soldier and an able administrator emerges with striking clarity; neither can his puritan sincerity or devoutness in matters of religious principle be held against him. On the other hand, he shared with the majority of his calling a peculiar lack of political expediency which caused him to recoil from the real issues undermining the close of the younger Cromwell's dislocated protectorate, so that when in 1659 Parliament and the army found themselves at loggerheads, he stepped bafflingly aside and failed to grasp the lead. Similarly, through a self-effacing loyalty to republicanism, he declined involvement in General Monck's quest for the return of the monarchy, putting his chances once and for all out of the running for position of state in the reconstituted order. In 1660, therefore, he retired from public life to the calm of his country estate of Feltwell in Norfolk where he remained until the early death of Bridget Cromwell in June 1662.

Bridget, not quite 38 years old, left her husband with two additional children as well as the guardianship of three daughters of her former marriage to Ireton. She was buried at St Anne's Blackfriars in the City of London, a church destroyed in the Great Fire of 1666 and never rebuilt; in this same church on 14 January 1664 Charles Fleetwood married his third wife, Dame Mary Hartopp of Newington, widow of the second Baronet and daughter of Sir John Coke. It was by this alliance that he came to take up residence in the house later identified with him at Stoke Newington, bringing with him no less than seven youngsters ranging in age from twenty downwards. In such a situation romance was bound to flourish and the newly acquired step-children, Sir John Hartopp and his sister Mary, were destined in 1666 for a double marriage with Fleetwood's two eldest offspring by his first wife, Smith and Elizabeth, so rendering the lines of Hartopp and Fleetwood inextricably fused. Because this was by far the largest house in the district, assessed for taxation purposes at twenty-five hearths in the period 1662-89, it proved able to accommodate the multiple family with ease and comfort. There was sufficient room for guests too, for among those frequently drawn by the amicable piety of the Stoke Newington retreat was the eminent Independent minister Dr John Owen (1616-1683) with whom Fleetwood had struck up an enduring friendship some time before 1651 when Owen preached at General Ireton's funeral. Rejecting his earlier inclinations towards Presbyterianism, Owen had embraced the Independents on taking the Essex incumbency of Coggeshall in the 1640s and proceeded to form his church there on Congregational principles. Already known for his polemical writings, he was brought to greater prominence as chaplain to Lord Fairfax in the siege of Colchester and summoned to Westminster to preach before Parliament on the day after the King's execution in January 1649. So impressed was Cromwell that he insisted upon Owen's company during his long excursions firstly to Ireland and immediately afterwards, joined by Fleetwood as Lieutenant General of the

Horse, to Scotland, scene of the Battle of Dunbar in 1650. Appointed Vice-Chancellor of Oxford University under Cromwell in 1652, Owen created a stir by scorning the customary formalities and dress of office in this most conservative of institutions, but in 1657 he retreated to London where early the following year he set up his own Independent church. Fleetwood was an original member, and the Hartopps came also to attend Dr Owen's church so that it was perhaps in these circumstances that the Lieutenant General became acquainted with his future third wife and her young family.

In the same neighbourhood as Owen's another Independent church was to be established by the Rev Joseph Caryl, former Rector of St Magnus the Martyr, London Bridge, whence he was ejected after the 1662 Act of Uniformity. Preaching at first in his own house in Bury Street, he gathered a congregation which afterwards met in nearby Leadenhall Street; in 1668 his daughter Sarah married Thomas Abney, a young dissenter heading for power in the financial undertakings of the City during William of Orange's reign. After Joseph Caryl's death in 1673 his numerous communicants united with the select congregation of Dr Owen, so creating the forerunner of the celebrated Mark Lane church. When Owen himself died in 1683 he was solemnly laid to rest in the Dissenters' Burial Ground recently established at Bunhill Fields, north of Moorgate. David Clarkson, his former assistant, was shortly replaced as pastor by the Rev Isaac Loeffs, during whose charge the church removed to Mark Lane, off Fenchurch Street. Loeffs gave way in 1687 to Dr Isaac Chauncey, an ineffective preacher superseded at the turn of the century by that great luminary of the Independents, Isaac Watts.

During the Commonwealth both Fleetwood and Owen had been closely associated with Dr Thomas Manton (1620-1677); reckoned among the principal and most popular nonconformist preachers of his time he was one of Cromwell's chaplains, Rector of Stoke Newington 1645-57, then Rector of St Paul Covent Garden until ejected in 1662. Afterwards imprisoned as an active dissenter he passed his latter years in semi-retirement, giving occasional lectures at Pinners' Hall in the City. Significantly he chose to be buried at his old parish church of Stoke Newington in 1677, and indeed the moral comradeship which bound Fleetwood and the Hartopps with Manton, Owen and his successors confirmed Stoke Newington as one of the chief centres of dissent in the second half of the the seventeenth century, with Fleetwood House its undoubted focus. The odd relationship in which these eminent nonconformists placed themselves vis à vis the establishment is well illustrated by Sir John Hartopp's refusal to serve as churchwarden when invited by the parish vestry in 1682. Uncompromising as an MP, he attracted adverse attention to his family by supporting the Exclusion Bill of 1685 designed to bar the Duke of York's accession to the throne as a Roman Catholic; its failure meant inevitable persecution once James II had secured his position and the year following, Hartopp, in company with Charles and Smith Fleetwood, suffered a heavy fine under the Act for the Suppression of Seditious Conventicles. Outside of the City of London, fearlessly independent in its support of dissent, it was not advisable until the Toleration Act of 1689 for nonconformist meeting-houses to advertise their existence, so although the Congregationalists of Stoke Newington (now represented by the Abney United Reformed Church) may trace their foundation to the year 1662, nothing is revealed of a permanent place of meeting until the 1690s, a decade of significant change within the parish.

Dame Mary Fleetwood had died on 17 December 1684 and was interred near the southern edge of the Dissenters' Burial Ground; Charles Fleetwood, in surviving the turbulence of James II's reign, no doubt gratefully welcomed the 1689 Revolution as prelude to an age of tolerance. He died at the age of 74 on 4 October 1692 leaving instructions for his own burial beside his third wife: their monument, a baroque chest tomb, was rediscovered seven feet below ground and restored by the City Corporation in 1869 when Bunhill Fields reopened as a public garden. With Fleetwood gone and the Lord of the Manor more remote than ever, it was left largely to the initiative of newcomers to bring fresh impetus to the district.

Needless to say these consisted of a new generation of nonconformists with Sir John Hartopp providing a vital link. The imperceptible arrival of Thomas Gunston (1667-1700) may be considered to date from 1681 when his father, John Gunston, a London linen draper of some prominence, took on official duties as a leading resident although he was merely tenant of a house standing astride an orchard in Church Street. However, by the spring of 1688 it seems John Gunston had already died leaving 20-year-old Thomas, the only surviving son, heir to a considerable fortune and responsibility for his sister Mary, then aged about 12. His first action was to purchase a large old house with three acres of grounds, formerly owned by the mercantile family of John Harris but until 1687 occupied by another City merchant, John Gould. This mansion, destined to remain Gunston's home from 1688 until his untimely death, stood on the south side of Church Street directly facing a small house attached to some sixty acres of meadowlands lying northward of the partially built-up road, mostly between Lordship Lane and Stamford Hill. Acquired by Thomas Gower in 1672 from Thomas Terry, whose forebears had retained their copyhold since James I's reign, these lands had come into the equal possession of Gower's two grand-daughters Elizabeth Gould and Anne Rutland by 1690 when Thomas Arnold of Stoke Newington bought out Elizabeth's interests. Young Gunston certainly had ambition in mind when, later the same year, he invested in the whole of Anne Rutland's portion. The new owners then

Garden Front Abney House, Stoke Newington, July 24 1843

7 Gunston's House, the entrance front, drawn by T H Shepherd in 1843. There is no historical consistency in the name of this house, which was at various times referred to as Gunston's or Lady Abney's House, the Mansion House or Manor House. In the early-nineteenth century it was usually one or other of the latter, but sometimes Abney Mansion too. Only in 1840 was the title Abney House first used.

arrived at an agreement in 1694 by which their respective shares would be rearranged as two separate flanking estates, Arnold taking the house and the westernmost lands bounded by Lordship Lane and Gunston the eastern chunks stretching across to Stamford Hill above Hartopp's grounds. He ended up with a main enclosure of seventeen acres partly skirted by Hackney Brook, together with the site of an adjoining tenement and orchard; a ten-acre field between brook and highway on Stamford Hill; as well as a detached four-acre meadow afterwards known as Gunston's Little Field on the north-eastern extremity of the manor lands: over thirty-one acres in all. Gunston's land had a clear but narrow frontage to Church Street beyond a huddle of tenements and **4** outbuildings at the west side of Fleetwood House, and so here in 1695 he planned to build a new mansion of greater pretensions in accord with his **7** wealth and standing. Disregarding his nonconformity, the Stoke Newington vestry nominated him in 1695 for parish office, a routine honour which Gunston declined on the excuse of uncertain health and, quite reasonably, because he was deeply involved in preparations for building his new home. His transition, brief though it proved to be, marks the real foundation of the Abney Estate developed under his immediate heirs and the not impartial eye of his intimate friend Dr Watts in the first half of the eighteenth century. At the precise moment of Gunston's domestic venture in 1695 the younger Alexander, grandson of Colonel Popham and absentee successor to the manorial properties, had the redundant Manor House demolished to make way for a smart new development. The ground was leased out, carved into lots, and between this date and 1709 a fine terrace of brick houses known as Church Row appeared on its site, one of them being reserved solely for official manor business. As his own splendid house drew towards realisation in 1699 Thomas Gunston capped his achievements with the outright purchase of the manor leasehold, so bringing to a close Alexander Popham's ancestral connexions of well over a century.

Isaac Watts DD (1674-1748) first made his appearance in Stoke Newington at

8 The Cedar of Lebanon, lithograph from a drawing by George Childs 1840 for George Collison's Cemetery Interment. Abney Mansion appears on the left.

the Rev Thomas Rowe's Nonconformist Academy on Newington Green, where he completed his education during the years 1690-94. Recalled from his native Southampton by Sir John Hartopp two and a half years later he was invited to live at Fleetwood House as resident tutor to Hartopp's son and heir John. Watts arrived on 15 October 1696; although the budding young poet and hymnwriter effortlessly established himself in this elite society of dissenters, a characteristic reserve kept him from preaching his first sermon until his twenty-fourth birthday, 17 July 1698. Among the earliest of his new acquaintances were Thomas and Sarah Abney, then living at Highgate Hill; also Nathaniel Gould, son-in-law of Sir John Hartopp, who had moved into Fleetwood House soon after the Lieutenant General's death and was responsible for its large westward extension in 1698-1700. Had it not been for Watts' presence, his youthful literary flights and a keen eye for his surroundings, little enough might have been recorded of the formative years of Abney Park. As it stands his early poetry, much of it arising from his stay at Fleetwood House, provides informative glimpses into the character both of the landscape and some of the people who inhabited it, while his subsequent fame as philosopher, theologian and a father of the English hymn has resulted in a rich store of legend centred on his eventual home. Physically slight, reticent and constitutionally delicate, the young tyro found himself lionised by a charmed circle of cultured merchant princes. Thomas Abney MP (1640-1722), Alderman and sometime Sheriff of London, was one of the original promoters of the Bank of England in 1694 and remained a Director of the Bank from its inception in that year. Afterwards knighted for his services to King William III, he was elected Lord Mayor of London for 1700-01, an office demanding at least occasional conformity to the Church of England. As a puritan therefore, Abney made himself an easy target of the pamphleteers for his dalliance with the establishment – Sir Tom would have been better employed singing psalms at Highgate Hill! Daniel Defoe, one of Stoke Newington's most distinguished literary figures, could not resist a gibe at the anomaly of his fellow dissenter's situation. Abney's younger colleague Nathaniel Gould MP (1661-1728), heir to the Fleetwood Estate, carried on business as a Turkey merchant in the City, becoming a Director of the Bank of England in 1697 and eventually Governor 1711-13; he was rewarded with a knighthood in 1721. His relative Edward Gould, another rich City magnate, had inherited by his marriage to Elizabeth Gower of Highgate an interest in the Stoke Newington lands and it was through his agency that Thomas Gunston had acquired the basis of his own new estate. These then formed the class of people to whom Watts ministered when he embarked on his pastoral career as Dr Chauncey's assistant early in 1699.

But it was to Gunston above all that Watts was most closely drawn. In more

9 Gate of Abney House in Church Street

dangerous times Gunston's father had attached himself to the dissenting cause and befriended many of the persecuted ministers; such was his excellent repute that Thomas Manton was even allowed out of prison to visit him. The son seems to have carried a family trait into the tolerant atmosphere of the 1690s; Watts and Gunston quickly became inseparable companions and spent pleasant hours dreaming up plans for the future. Watts was willingly caught up in the great house-building project next door, while the two neighbouring estates, freely explored by this oddly complementary pair, became transfigured by their minds' eye into a splendid stately park. Indeed, the makings of it were already there in the form of rows of mature elms planted earlier in the seventeenth century, a veritable wilderness of a shrubbery screening off the north side of Fleetwood gardens and, by its side, a shapely Cedar of Lebanon **8** planted according to tradition in the Lieutenant General's time and which miraculously survived into the early-twentieth century. Forming a natural curb to Gunston's grounds on the north, the Hackney Brook took a sharp loop southward on the eastern flank around a remote ornamental mound, surrounding it completely and picturesquely by water; here was a heronry, **11** which could be reached along the Fleetwood boundary through a long straggling orchard. The Mansion itself was planned to face proudly into a deep **7** entrance courtyard, revealed towards Church Street through a graceful wrought iron gateway and railings set between high brick walls. Gunston **9** went on to improve his frontage with the purchase of tenement gardens on the east side in 1698, so by then at latest he was ready to build the house. Its style was both handsome and restrained in a manner typical of the larger City merchants' palaces of William III's reign, rising cleanly rectangular in good red brick with a dominating slated mansard roof framed by tall regular chimneys. This basic severity of profile was relieved by a trim balustrade round the top of the roof, beyond which rose a particularly pretty central lantern with bell-shaped cupola – a glazed octagonal lookout – all topped off with a glittering golden sphere. South and north, entrance and garden fronts were identical **10** two-storey compositions of seven bays with tall rectangular windows arranged symmetrically about a central door, that of the principal entrance distinguished by a carved shell hood. Contained within the deep eaved roof an attic storey received light by square dormer windows under alternating triangular and curved pediments.

Solid and square it rises from below:
A noble air without a gaudy show
Reigns thro' the model, and adorns the whole,
Manly and plain. Such was the builder's soul.

Certainly it must have presented an edifying corrective to the somewhat random appearance of its old neighbour Fleetwood House, then itself undergoing a major facelift, but alas the architect has passed unrecorded. Gunston intended that his chief rooms should be richly painted with murals, and some at least had been carried out by the end of 1700. One of the upper front rooms, afterwards known as the Painted Room, had large gilt panels ornamented with subjects from Ovid's *Metamorphoses*, that over the chimney-piece displaying the Transformation of Actaeon into a stag with a lake in the foreground. Aside from his deep learning and piety, Isaac Watts was evidently not without a wry sense of humour when, while the artist was at dinner, he completed the watery scene by painting in a swan.

The pity is that Gunston never saw his enterprise concluded. He had complained of unreliable health as early as 1695, but after one brief year as Lord of the Manor the warnings clearly became insistent causing him to renew his lease and place all his property in trust with a kinsman, John Gunston (*c*1660-1728). He appears to have been equally anxious to marry off his sister and heir Mary, then at the age of twenty-four, for on 21 August 1700 she became second wife to Sir Thomas Abney, widowed two years previously and no less than thirty-six years her senior. By late autumn Gunston had fallen seriously ill; on 11 November 1700 all plans for the wealthy young man came to an abrupt end. In his thirty-fourth year he was dead.

Gunston the just, the generous, and the young,
Gunston the friend, is dead. O empty name
Of earthly bliss! 'tis all an airy dream,
All a vain thought! our soaring fancies rise
On treacherous wings! and hopes that touch the skies
Drag but a longer ruin through the downward air,
And plunge the fallen joy still deeper in despair.

The solemn and elaborate funeral followed on 22 November, an appropriately gloomy day of leaden skies and fitful downpours, when with all the pompous embellishments of mourning Thomas Gunston was borne to his chilly vault beneath St Mary's Church. Plans for his reputed forthcoming marriage to Mary, one of the elder daughters of Sir John Hartopp, thus came to naught and she remained at Fleetwood House where she died a spinster in 1748. Watts exorcised his grief in a deeply touching Pindaric Elegy (from which the above two quotations are taken) remarkable still for its vivid topographical and emotive allusions, if not for any great originality of form. It was above all a private outpouring meant in the first instance for his own solace, then later at her request for Mary, Lady Abney, to whom the poem was dedicated as Lady Mayoress of London in July 1701. After a decent interval Watts published it in his *Horae Lyricae* of 1706 and it may come as some surprise to anyone familiar

10 Abney House from the park, lithograph from a drawing by G Childs 1840 for Collison's Cemetery Interment.

only with the memorable hymns for which he is now most honoured. Who for instance does not know *Our God, Our Help in Ages past*. This, his undoubted masterpiece, and many others beside, took the religious world by storm when they first appeared; their holy fire coupled with elegance of language helped revolutionise the outward expression of nonconformity making it a cultural force to be reckoned with. On the other hand such autobiographical statements as the early Gunston Elegy allow a more personal view of this remarkably versatile man.

By Gunston's will, Lady Abney inherited all of her brother's property and thus by right of marriage Sir Thomas Abney became joint Lord of the Manor in 1701. Watts gloomily illustrated the succession by painting on the deserted Mansion's window-shutters emblems of Death and Time, Strength Destroyed, and Life Poured Out, with the Gunston arms in mourning and the City arms in crape. At a later date, and evidently in lighter mood, he decorated two of the parlours with characters of Youth and Age, Mirth and Grief. Sir Thomas however owned a town house in the City and was about to exchange Highgate Hill for a large summer residence at Theobalds Park near Cheshunt;

so the Stoke Newington estate remained in trust. John Gunston set about
9 finishing off the entrance gateway and other subsidiary works at Thomas's
Mansion in 1701; both eastern and western party walls were settled and
completed that same year. It is most likely that he made his home there during
this period but in later years he let it, together with the seventeen-acre
grounds, to the engagingly eccentric Thomas Cooke (c1672-1752), son-in-law
of Sir Nathaniel Gould and like him a Turkey merchant, Director of the Bank of
England from 1721 then latterly Governor in 1737-40. Meanwhile Isaac Watts
had succeeded Dr Chauncey as pastor of Mark Lane Church in 1702, removing
somewhat reluctantly from the Hartopp household to a lodging in the
Minories. He was kept busy as the replenished congregation shortly removed
successively to Pinners' Hall 1704, then to a new chapel in Bury Street near
Aldgate in 1708. Nonetheless, he maintained close associations with Stoke
Newington and was frequently called upon to preach in the new Independent
chapel (precursor of Abney Chapel) erected in 1700 on the north side of Church
Street, near Edwards Lane, to replace an earlier meeting-house pulled down
for the construction of Gunston's stables. When Lady Elizabeth Hartopp and
her daughter Frances Gould died within a few days of each other in 1711,
Watts paid them tribute in a funeral sermon at this chapel, little guessing that
within a year he would find himself in the grips of a severe breakdown, the
effects of which were to dog him for the remainder of his life:

> *Oh 'tis all confusion!*
> *If I but close my eyes, strange images*
> *In thousand forms and thousand colours rise –*
> *Stars, rainbows, moons, green dragons, bears and ghosts.*

As he slowly recovered in the spring of 1714, Sir Thomas Abney urged Watts
to spend a week with his family in the fresh air and pleasant country of
Theobalds Park. It turned out a fateful convalescence, for Watts was graciously
drawn into the Abney household and never again left it. When he needed to be
in town he stayed at their City house in Lime Street, but until the early 1730s
Theobalds was his home. With the death of Sir Thomas on 6 February 1722 (he
was buried in the Abney vault at St Peter Cornhill), the manor responsi-
bilities fell entirely to Lady Mary although another twelve years were to pass
before she came to live on her brother's estate. Changes had taken place at
Fleetwood House too. Sir John Hartopp had died in 1722 – his funeral
occasioned Watts' celebrated discourse on *The Happiness of Separate Spirits* –
and the poet's former pupil Sir John Hartopp, fourth and last Baronet (1682-
1762), was less directly involved in nonconformist circles after his father's
death. He had in any case already departed from London to look after his
country estates, although his friendship towards Lady Abney and Watts

always remained warm. Thomas Cooke and his wife had the pleasure of Gunston's Mansion from 1721 until Sir Nathaniel Gould's death in 1728 when they inherited and moved into a much improved Fleetwood House; then too John Gunston died but not before completing the sale of the ten-acre field on Stamford Hill and the adjacent island mound. Gould himself had bought them **4** in three separate instalments over the years 1712-26 as part of his gradual expansion of the Fleetwood property, so all this now belonged to Cooke. As for Gunston's old residence across the street, hitherto let to one Charles Gery, it was sold in 1729 to the Cole family of Magdalen Laver who, through successive deaths, had allowed it to fall into decay and ruin by 1732. On finally sorting out his complicated inheritance, Henry Cole the younger demolished the shattered building to erect in its place, in 1733-35, a handsome terrace of four brick houses with a central archway leading to yards behind. This group still remains complete as 81-87 Church Street, opposite Clarence Terrace.

As a widow, Lady Abney maintained family life at Theobalds with her three daughters and Isaac Watts, although her second daughter, Mary Pickard (c1703-1738) shortly married and moved away. After the early death of Sarah Abney (c1702-1732), the eldest daughter, Theobalds Park may well have seemed too big, for in 1734 it was given up and the move made to Stoke Newington. Lady Mary with her third daughter Elizabeth and Dr Watts (he had received an Honorary Doctorate of Divinity from the University of Edinburgh in 1728) installed themselves in Gunston's Mansion; a survey of the demesne lands was ordered by the Lady of the Manor in 1734, then she set about putting her grounds in order. Watts, with his wide-ranging cultural interests, has been credited with some of the planting in the park, in particular the later of two stately avenues of elms which lined the walks northward from **11** the gardens, although his part in this is by no means certain. It is likely, however, that he may have been responsible for a fine old horse-chestnut tree formerly crowning the island mound in Hackney Brook; although taken as part of Cooke's property, this mound at the end of the long orchard became to Watts a favourite refuge where he could meditate in seclusion. By the early-nineteenth century a curious mythology had grown up around Watts' famous **20** retreat which related that it contained Oliver Cromwell's body transported from Westminster Abbey and secretly reinterred, when the Restoration of the Monarchy became inevitable, to secure it from certain defilement. Alas, the lugubrious tale rested entirely on the false supposition that Bridget Cromwell lived here with her husband Fleetwood during the Commonwealth – and so the romantic aura of the Mount (to use a Victorian euphemism) is adequately dispelled by Watts' own explanation of its old purpose as 'a very agreeable piece of elevated ground whence could be surveyed the neighbouring fields and meadows covered with cattle.' He, clearly, was not familiar with the legend.

Isaac Watts lived at the Abney Park Mansion from 1734, when he was at the peak of his fame, until his death within its walls on 25 November 1748 aged seventy-four. In youth the intimate friend of its builder, he saw the great house take shape from a position of privilege; he returned to it at length the revered companion of the sister and niece. Towards the end when his mind became fitfully clouded by monstrous hallucinations, Lady Abney so adroitly shielded him from intrusions that his early biographers were unaware of his sad state. According to his wishes he was interred in Bunhill Fields, the interminably ceremonious funeral taking place on 5 December 1748; here during the following year a stone chest tomb was placed over his grave as the joint testimonial of Lady Abney and Sir John Hartopp. Not long passed before Lady Mary Abney herself died on 12 January 1750 at the age of about seventy-three; she was buried near her brother beneath the chancel of Stoke Newington Church. Elizabeth Abney (c1704-1782), the youngest daughter, inherited both the Abney estate and the manor lease in 1750. Previously, in 1740, she had invested in some copyhold land on her own account by acquiring a square orchard on the south of Church Street directly opposite the gate of
4 Abney Mansion. This orchard, abutting the site of Gunston's first house on the west, now became part of the estate but later during her charge, after 1765, the remote 'Little Field' of four acres near Woodberry Down was leased out as farmland eventually to be absorbed into the manor demesnes. As the last Abney to hold the manor Elizabeth remained a spinster, carrying on the traditions of her family without the slightest change; even her mode of dress was remarkable for its archaism. She died aged seventy-eight on 20 August 1782, her will directing that all should be sold and the proceeds, after certain bequests, divided between various nonconformist charities.

By 1766 the Hartopps and their relatives had all died or departed from Fleetwood House leaving it split into two separate residences. It was then sold complete to George Perrott, Baron of the Exchequer, who lived in the western section of the house from 1763 until his retirement in 1775. Nathaniel Gould's substantial extension, for which he cleared away properties grouped at the west of the old house in 1698, was presumably built in a more up-to-date manner than the rest and no doubt resulted in a quaintly picturesque juxtapositon of styles. Now Perrott acceded to a thorough modernisation which, between 1766-69, transformed the whole exterior into a red brick
5 Palladian mansion while retaining the anomoly of its former lopsided
6 composition. Perrott's heirs sold the Fleetwood estate in 1797 to the Robley family, already in occupation as tenants for some ten years. Their representative, Mrs Ann Robley, left the house only in 1824 leasing it to a Quaker Girls' School which flourished here under the administration of Miss Susanna

Corder for the next fourteen years, although the Robleys sold up the whole property in 1827.

The manor and the Abney estate had been put up for auction on 26 May 1783; together they fetched £13,000 with another £583 for furniture and effects. The highest bidder was Jonathan Eade (1745-1811), a Wapping ship chandler who in *c*1770 had married Margaret, daughter of John Bowles, the Cornhill printseller and publisher then living in retirement in a large early-eighteenth century house in Stoke Newington. On Bowles' death in 1779, Eade and his family moved into this house on the south side of Church Street (still standing as Nos 109-111), but as lessee of the manor from 1783 he took up residence in Abney Mansion subsequently making various alterations to the rooms. By the time of Eade's purchase the grounds, which according to the printed particulars of sale comprised just under twenty-two acres inclusive both of the house and the orchard opposite, had matured to a state of proverbial beauty. North of the house, five acres were laid out as gardens, lawns and pleasure **10** grounds, including a bowling green. There was also a small farmyard to the west, very likely on the site of an old tenement, to which separate access opened from Church Street alongside the west party wall. Above this, and following the long section of the western boundary, an ornamental water-course or canal had been cut to connect up with Hackney Brook on the north. Jonathan Eade was the last Lord of the Manor to occupy this idyllic place; he died on 26 September 1811 and was buried on the east side of Stoke Newington Churchyard where his family tomb may still be seen. The joint heirs were his two surviving sons, William (*c*1775-1825) and Joseph (1781-1828)) who, while retaining their manor interests, lived away from Stoke Newington and so offered the Abney copyhold for sale. Their mother, Margaret Eade, removed in 1812 to the Summerhouse, just east of Fleetwood's gardens, where she died in 1824.

The estate was now divided up: two large western closes totalling ten acres which lay alongside the canal between farmyard and brook were sold for £3,000 in 1813, and the west side of the farm went with them. John Bond, their purchaser, incorporated these portions into his own estate, part of the former Arnold lands next door with a house rebuilt in 1790, which he had acquired in 1806. Then in 1813-14 the Mansion with its remaining long strip of grounds went for £4,500 to J W Freshfield, solicitor to the Bank of England; he paid another £1,000 for the orchard opposite. During his ownership from 1814 to 1838 Freshfield, who evidently cared much for the place, removed Eade's alterations and restored the interior of Gunston's house to something approaching its original condition. He also embarked on major replanting works in the grounds. When Bond sold up and moved to Bath in 1824, Freshfield and his son rescued the two western closes and farmyard for a reduced bid of £2,000 to reassemble the estate in its eighteenth century form. Further, in 1827, they obtained from the Robley trustees the whole of **11** Fleetwood House and its original land, together with the island in the brook. This all cost them another £3,750 but after a full century of partition Watts' mound had regained its rightful status in Abney Park. In the same transaction, however, the Robleys detached the ten-acre field on Stamford Hill and sold it **21** for £2,300 to a speculator, Thomas Maughan of Clerkenwell.

William and Joseph Eade, as joint Lords of the Manor, had astutely prepared the way for Stoke Newington's development as a prospering London suburb and negotiated a new lease with the Cathedral Authorities in 1814 incorporating privileges of enfranchisement and new land use. This, with an Act of Parliament in the same year, meant that copyhold properties could be converted to freehold ownership: brickfields would rapidly develop and speculative housing soon follow. After this the impact of the manor lessees dwindled; by 1820 William Eade had sold his interests to his younger brother and later went abroad. He died in Bordeaux in 1825. Joseph Eade died at his home in Hitchin in 1828 but found his last resting place in the family vault at Stoke Newington; henceforth the Eade trustees carried on manor business in consort but were gradually reduced to a legal cipher. In 1840-41 the prebendal properties were handed over to the Ecclesiastical Commissioners who eventually, in 1882, purchased the remaining lessees' rights.

11 Plan of the combined Abney and Fleetwood Estate in 1838, drawing from the conveyance document of 1839. Fleetwood House has been separated from the estate and walled off immediately to the east of Abney Mansion (commonly, as here, called the Manor House). The Cedar of Lebanon is shown beside an ornamental pond north of Fleetwood's gardens and near a line of yew trees. Further north-eastwards Hackney Brook cuts off the detached Ten Acre Field before disappearing beneath Stamford Bridge at the eastern extremity of the grounds. Near the centre of Abney estate the Great Elm Walk is clearly marked bordering the two western closes and farmyard retrieved from John Bond's sale in 1824. The long orchard leading to Dr Watts' Mound had by this time receded to the north.

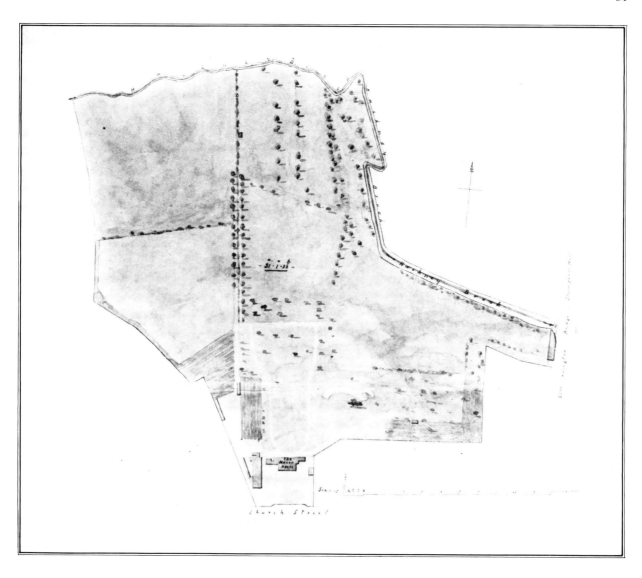

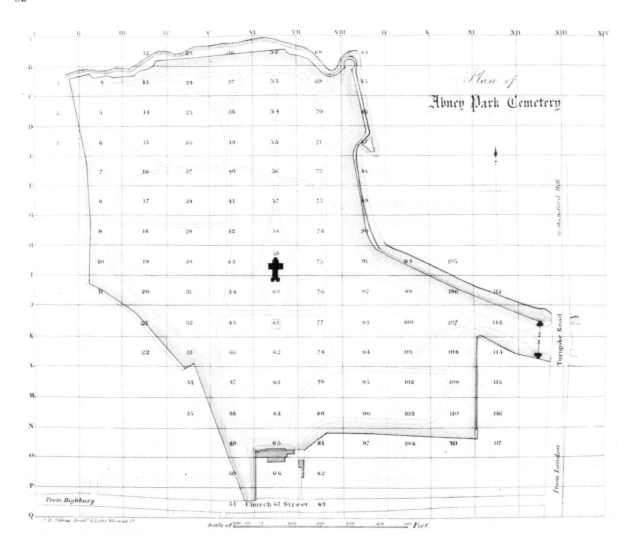

Plan of
Abney Park Cemetery

The Cemetery
planning, building and planting

12 Plan of Abney Park Cemetery in 1840, lithograph by J R Jobbins for Collison's Cemetery Interment. The original pattern of routes shown here did not include Dr Watts' Walk, Cedar Path or New Road; and Abney House is walled off from the cemetery grounds. Boundary walls are marked on the inner banks of Hackney Brook on the north and north-east. Comparison with the estate plan of 1838 will reveal that many of the old features were carried over to the new layout.

Before 1821 there were no proper public cemeteries at all in Great Britain; that is, apart from such specialised instances as Bunhill Fields in London (established 1665), Clifton Graveyard in Belfast (founded 1774), and Calton Hill Cemetery, Edinburgh (in use by 1778). But these three had been created in response to the particular needs of traditionally nonconformist communities whose liberal ethics placed them outside the influence of the establishment. The old Jewish burial grounds too were products of a similar situation and much the same might have been said of that strangely obscure pioneer of English nineteenth century cemeteries, The Rosary in Norwich, founded by a dissenting minister in memory of his wife in 1821, were it not that it never catered exclusively for nonconformist interment. The modern public cemetery movement emerged as a somewhat tardy by-product of the Age of Enlightenment in hand with the Industrial Revolution and was brought into being to cope with huge population expansions prompted by the rapid technological progress. As urban reform had then to be tackled on a scale hitherto undreamt of, it became clear at once that a radical approach to burial of the dead would have to be devised.

Curiously, however, it was not in industrialised England but in Napoleonic France that the first great garden cemeteries were planned. Père-Lachaise overlooking Paris, the earliest and most influential of all, was laid out from 1804 onwards and still remains among the most impressive pieces of artificial landscape of its kind anywhere. Nothing in England was ever likely to exceed the vast scale or grandeur of this Parisian cemetery, although North America took up the French theme with alacrity at Mount Auburn Cemetery near Boston in 1831 and pressed on to expand the form in characteristic opulence throughout the remainder of the century. After Norwich Rosary, initially slow to be recognised as a public amenity as it attracted no more than a dozen or so interments during the first half-decade of its existence, the earliest significant British developments occurred in the industrial north. At Liverpool the Necropolis Cemetery, founded under dissenting influence, was opened in 1825; the City's conformist interests made swift response with St James'

Cemetery, nearer the centre of Liverpool, dramatically laid out in a disused quarry during 1825-29. These were perhaps modest beginnings in comparison with the Napoleonic achievement, but once grasped the principle quickly resolved into a major public issue. Taking its cue from Père-Lachaise, the spectacular Necropolis of Glasgow was the creation of an enlightened Presbyterian regime in 1828-32, but made free to all religious parties. Dublin also shortly received its two splendid early cemeteries, Protestant and Catholic respectively, in 1832.

Although its need was perhaps most urgent of all, London had lagged unbelievably behind the provinces in this pressing reform, for in spite of the pitifully squalid state of its old burial grounds no practical attempt to relieve them materialised until 1830. The multiplicity of cramped city churchyards particularly, with their impossible ancient burdens, had long been a scandal and a disgrace to the capital, for quite apart from their appalling neglect and decay they had become a prevailing threat to both health and adjacent property. Such cynical disregard for the means of disposing of the dead outraged the moral sensibilities of a handful of dedicated reformers who publicised their concern in no uncertain terms in the journals of the 1820s. London, they pronounced, was shamed by the examples of Paris and Liverpool but the needs of the masses would have to be recognised. In 1830 the eminent Scottish landscape gardener, John Claudius Loudon (1783-1843), first published his own independent proposals for a series of cemeteries to surround London which would, in addition, be laid out as botanical gardens for the pleasure and instruction of visitors. Although he died relatively early in Victoria's reign, Loudon's influence reached forward, through his numerous botanical textbooks and other publications, well beyond the later Victorian decades in the design of gardens, arboreta and, most visibly still, in suburban landscape of all kinds.

During the ten years 1831-1841 the campaign, led by a barrister, George Frederick Carden, produced seven spacious and magnificent cemeteries laid out by private enterprise to encircle the suburbs of London. The initial outcome, directly under Carden's influence, was the promotion of the General Cemetery Company in 1830; they created Kensal Green Cemetery in 1831-33 and it rapidly became one of the sights of London. Kensal Green proved so commercially successful that it encouraged the formation of other London cemetery companies within three years of its opening. Norwood Cemetery, 1836-37, and Highgate Cemetery 1836-39, proceeded in rapid succession; Brompton in 1838-40, then Abney Park and Nunhead both in 1839-40; lastly Tower Hamlets brought up the rearguard in 1840-41. These ambitious projects were all established by joint-stock companies incorporated, with the singular exception of the Abney Park Cemetery Company, by individual Acts of

Parliament. They later inspired the 1852 Burial Act empowering local vestries to set up Burial Boards for the provision of their own municipal cemeteries outside metropolitan limits, most of which were based on rather different standards from the independent early seven. However, the vast City of London Cemetery at Little Ilford, laid out for the City Corporation in 1854-56, is a particularly splendid exception to the modest rule adopted for a large majority of the municipal cemeteries following from the 1852 Act. Neither did the spirit of private enterprise entirely evaporate, but because its monopoly was effectively exploded by the Act, some of the more imaginative later commercial schemes, like the excellent Great Northern Cemetery at New Southgate of 1861, never fulfilled their original intentions.

Strategically grouped around the south-west, west and north of London, the first four of the seven great cemeteries left the less opulent south-east and north-eastern sectors still unprovided for by 1838. In the early part of that year a City of London solicitor, George Collison, carried out investigation of the most recent annual burial statistics throughout the City and north-east London with a view to justify a new cemetery foundation within the area. He must surely have been aware that the London Cemetery Company, constituted by Act of Parliament in 1836, had already formed tentative plans for an East London burial ground but its prime objective for the moment consisted only of the laying out of Highgate Cemetery; later when the Abney Park scheme looked like succeeding, the senior company turned its attention to the south-east and purchased the Nunhead ground. Of the urgent need for such an establishment in the north-east ample evidence emerged as the returns for the year 1837 amounted to some nine thousand, the majority doubtless sent off to an uneasy rest in overflowing, unsanitary parish churchyards. Although little enough is known of him, Collison, son of the Rev George Collison (1772-1847), President of Hackney Congregational Theological College, appears to have been the grey eminence behind the Abney Park Cemetery project for, as both Secretary and Registrar to the Company from 1839 onwards, he was certainly its earliest publicist as well as its original historian. Mysteriously overlooked by nearly all modern cemetery investigators, his book entitled *Cemetery Interment*, written and published during 1840, contains a loaded critical assessment of the public burial movement up to that time culminating, most appropriately, in an expansive discourse upon the superior advantages of the new and rather different cemetery at Stoke Newington, then **13** not long opened. Even though this remarkable piece of advertising remains the prime source of detailed information on the creation and original appearance of the cemetery, Collison declines to offer any indication of the other personalities involved in the enterprise, or of their possible connexions with the proprietor of the Abney and Fleetwood estates. The few existing early records of the Company – mostly legal documents – yield up their names however and, for several of them, their family tombs provide further enlightenment.

Apart from Collison then, who also acted as their law representative, the founders were nine in number. Typical of the majority in their calling as successful City magnates and financiers, Thomas Kelly of Paternoster Row, an Alderman of London, and Thomas Merriman Coombs of Ludgate Street respectively head the list in all legal transactions although Josiah John Luntley of Hackney possessed additional practical advantage to the group in that his kinsman, W Luntley of Shoreditch (later installed at Bishopsgate), ran a well-established business as an undertaker-cum-auctioneer. His services were to be widely utilised by the Company. Another member, John Hosking of Newington in South London, is worth mentioning if only for his palpable link with the architectural profession. These and others of their colleagues might be characterised as the rather less obviously picturesque heirs of the merchant princes of Restoration London, hard-headed middle-class protestant businessmen but at the same time men of conscience and high moral responsibility, adept at combining good works with the making of profit. In one instance only was there a public figure involved: he was the Rev James Sherman (1796-1862), successor to Rowland Hill as minister of Surrey

13 Panoramic view of the Cemetery, lithograph from a drawing by G Childs 1840, issued as a separate print to shareholders of the Abney Park Cemetery Company. The view looks north from the roof turret of Abney House towards the heights of Woodberry Down and Stamford Hill, depicted as still in rural splendour with the waters of the new reservoirs glistening through the trees. At the centre are the Catacombs and the as yet unbuilt Chapel; the Cedar of Lebanon figures prominently in the right foreground and beyond it can be made out the features of Dr Watts' Mound. Left of the Chapel is the imposing entrance to the Great Elm Walk. Solemn funeral processions complete the romantic atmosphere.

ABNEY PARK CEMETERY.

VIEW OF THE GROUNDS FROM Dr WATTS' TURRET ON ABNEY HOUSE.

Chapel, Blackfriars and a familiar nineteenth century type as the charismatic preacher converting the multitudes by his silver-tongued rhetoric. Most significantly of all perhaps, each of these gentlemen was of the Congregationalist persuasion, a fact which was to have far-reaching effects on the constitution, form and operation of the new establishment.

Collison's research had carried enough conviction for the group to take some positive action. In view of their religious affiliations it is not surprising that hopes should have been cast on the possibility of obtaining a site like the Abney-Fleetwood estate with its deep-rooted spiritual assets. Quite how the quarry was approached is now a matter for speculation but the City banking fraternity was, as it still remains, remarkably close-knit and some of the founders will have been well enough acquainted with James William Freshfield as a solicitor within the sphere of their professional activities. At any rate negotiations for the purchase of the consolidated estate went ahead **11** during the latter part of the year, culminating in the enfranchisement, or conversion to freehold, of the whole property by Freshfield on 20 December 1838; so too Fleetwood house, together with its immediate back gardens already walled off from the old grounds beyond, became separately enfranchised on the same date. Neither was this the first occasion upon which the present owner had taken advantage of the Eade Brothers' 1814 Act for in 1837 Freshfield enfranchised Elizabeth Abney's orchard opposite for its immediate freehold sale to trustees of Abney Meeting House. Here, some six years into the ministry of the Rev John Jefferson, they built in 1837-38 a capacious and handsome new chapel from designs of James Fenton of Chelmsford. Freshfield had moved out of Abney Mansion by early 1826, his tenants now leaving way for the nine new proprietors whose transaction was sealed on 30 January 1839 for the sum of £12,080.

All crucial decisions relating to the formation of the cemetery must have been taken during the course of 1838 as the members resolved their hitherto noncommital association into a joint-stock company, with themselves as its nine trustees, by a deed of covenant dated 11 February 1839, but retrospectively so that the legal obligations of the Abney Park Cemetery Company would cover their joint activities back to 14 May 1838. 'The object of this Company, is the establishment of a General Cemetery for the City of London and its eastern and north-eastern suburbs, which shall be open to all classes of the community and to all denominations of Christians without restraint in forms.' So ran the opening statement of a Prospectus issued by the trustees immediately after their covenant; it went on to advertise the constitution of the new company, its purposes and its financial arrangements. Capital stock consisted of £35,000 which was to be divided into 3,500 shares of £10 each; there was to be a maximum of nine trustees at any one time but the Company

14 Gates, lodges and forecourt, lithograph from a drawing by G Childs 1840 for Collison's Cemetery Interment.

would be run by a Board of Directors, some of whose number were also drawn from the founder-trustees. The cemetery was projected to satisfy the needs of the City of London and its eastern suburbs, not only for the wealthier mercantile or professional communities and superior tradesmen resident there but most particularly for the immense mass of the poor (ie the working class). Its catchment area was estimated to include, over and above the City and Tower Hamlets, Finsbury, Shoreditch, Hackney and Stoke Newington; in addition Tottenham, Edmonton and even Enfield would be expected to respond. At this stage the new cemetery foundation at Tower Hamlets had not been forseen but in the event it hardly affected the fortunes of Abney Park. Moreover, although Bunhill Fields still operated as a burial ground favoured by nonconformists, it had become so pitifully crammed, with the soil rising many feet above the pavements, that it was a mercy to close it against further interments in 1854. Indeed one of the functions of Abney Park itself was to serve as a renewed focus for dissenting burial, with the emphasis on Congregationalism as it turned out, and so preserve the venerable traditions of Bunhill Fields in more inspiriting surroundings.

The constitution of the Abney Park Cemetery Company was different from that of other recent cemeteries in that no special Act of Parliament was obtained and no Episcopal consecration of the grounds took place. Viewed as altogether objectionable encumbrances on the broad, liberal Christian principles by which the Company had determined to stand or fall, neither of these things could in their omission affect the stability or the legality of the institution. In this the example of Liverpool Necropolis was adhered to because, as the legal requirements for Kensal Green and the other London cemeteries sufficiently demonstrated, an individual Act of Parliament meant the imposition of exorbitant fees payable to the clergy of those parishes whence the dead had originated in order to make up their lost income from traditional burial rights. Far more seriously, it would have demanded consecration by a bishop of the Established Church, another unpalatable relic of medieval popery according to the dissenters and, furthermore, a ritual which possessed neither basis in law nor conferred any spiritual advantages on the interred. Entirely the reverse in truth for the terms then imposed would have defeated the object and scope of the cemetery as originally intended. All dissenters, and this included Jews and Roman Catholics, were ignominiously barred from burial in consecrated ground unless according to the rites of the Church of England and it was a declared aim that every portion of Abney Park Cemetery should be open to all parties without distinction or preference. Conscience dictated that no humiliating demarcations, such as had cordonned off the exiles in earlier cemeteries, should be allowed to mar this silent assembly of equals. It was a somewhat bold venture, but in the result the public appreciated and were prepared to support it: within one month of the Prospectus being issued the whole amount of capital was subscribed for, the shareholders numbering between two and three hundred and embracing episcopalians as well as dissenters of all denominations. As to the purchase of graves, Collison reproduces the original Scale of Charges as an appendix to his text and further states that every corpse is deposited in freehold ground, and that the proprietors of graves will have a distinct legal right to a perpetual interest in the fee.

After the success of the Prospectus, one of the first questions to be tackled was what to do with Abney Mansion, now standing forlorn and empty. Fortunately at first there was a prospective tenant so the great house was walled off **10** from the estate and became for a time host to the Wesleyan Theological Institution. Secondly the inclosure and drainage of thirty-one acres of grounds had to be put in hand: to this end a well-shaft was sunk twenty-five feet into the clay at the lower end of the site during the summer of 1839. It was left open for several months but the walls remained intact and no water seeped through. A well-borer then dipped twenty-five feet further down, again without sign of

11 flooding. The surface water, which included an ornamental pond by the Cedar of Lebanon as well as the inner course of Hackney Brook isolating Watts' mound, had to be run off by the new drainage system connected up with the Brook on the northern boundaries. Of constructed brick drains, there was built an aggregate length of one and three quarter miles; of cross and tile drains a total of nearly four miles. All this was achieved very swiftly. Substantial inclosure walls of stock brick were raised to an external height varying between ten and twelve feet above the sloping inner banks of the Brook but on the northern perimeter cast iron railings set between a succession of brick piers opened up for one hundred yards the delightful country view towards Woodberry Down. Elsewhere in the southern parts of the estate stretches of new walling were worked in with reconditioned

12 existing boundary walls. The general layout of the cemetery, including drives and paths, had to concur both with the courses required by the main drain channels and with the existing ornamental timber and shrubs, of which a large quantity was retained. Another important factor in the planning of routes was to provide the greatest possible extent of frontage for grave plots and easy access to all parts of the grounds. Taking each of these considerations into account, the picturesque irregularity of the site suggested an informal, asymmetric layout as most favourable but with strongly stressed leading features which could be arranged to converge at the approximate centre,

13 where eye-catching chapel and catacombs lie along the principal axis cutting northward from Abney Mansion. At the south side of Stamford Bridge, an old tenement still blocked off the highway from the narrow eastern arm of the

front cover Fleetwood estate but this was destined to make way for a grand formal entrance whose long carriage drive could be taken across in leisurely arcs to its terminus beneath the chapel's porte-cochère. Altogether nearly three miles of boundary roads and drives, with the first instalment of access paths, had been completed by the spring of 1840.

Who then was responsible for the planning of this highly artificial but romantic landscape? Its complete architectural arrangements, drainage, inclosure and disposition of the grounds, in a word all with the significant exception of the innovatory new planting scheme, had been placed in the hands of William Hosking FSA (1800-1861), from 1840 onwards Professor of Architecture and Civil Engineering at King's College, London but who so far as can be made out had never yet built more than a single purely architectural work. Born in Devon, Hosking had emigrated with his family to New South Wales in his ninth year; there in Sydney he was apprenticed to a builder-surveyor but on returning to England ten years later he became in 1820 pupil to a Wesleyan minister turned architect, the Rev William Jenkins of Red Lion Square, Holborn. Three years afterwards he travelled extensively in France,

Italy and Sicily, but little is recorded of his professional activities until 1834 when he was appointed Engineer to the new Bimingham, Bristol and Thames Junction Railway. For this Company he designed a complex arrangement of bridge and aqueduct near Kensal Green by which the Grand Union Canal was suspended over the West London Railway, and a road in turn over the canal. Constructed in 1838-39, this ingenious three-tier feat received wide acclaim and confirmed Hosking's reputation as an engineer. How he came by the Abney Park commission in early 1839 is not known but there were already several points in his favour. For a start he was apparently related to John Hosking of Surrey Square, Newington, one of the nine founder-trustees; also it is quite certain that he was himself a nonconformist by conviction and indeed his next job was to design Trinity Independent Chapel in Poplar, 1840-41 (now demolished). Then cemetery layout was generally considered a mainly engineering task although it was taken for granted that the engineer would be capable of turning out an architectural design in the appropriate style. No wonder that few of the more distinguished Victorian architects were tempted into the field. On top of these obvious qualifications, however, Hosking maintained good connexions in the affairs of archaeology, so that in a scheme to restore the great Bristol church of St Mary Redcliffe in 1842 the medievalist antiquarian John Britton was to be his colleague. It therefore comes as no surprise that he was able to call to his aid Joseph Bonomi junior, the distinguished Egyptologist, in devising the more arcane details of the Abney Park entrance ensemble.

Of a slighly earlier generation than the mainstream Victorian gothic revivalists, Hosking was hardly affected by the moralistic approach to design initiated by the young Pugin and the ecclesiological movement in the late 1830s. On the contrary, his engineering bias led him to favour an austere kind of stripped classicism, but he seems to have been equally happy to adopt rather more exotic styles when occasion demanded. Probably the only example of his architectural work now remaining, Abney Park demonstrates this flexibility to the utmost for his perimeter walls have thin neoclassical features surmounting their buttress piers, the chapel is predictably gothic with some obvious borrowings from identifiable early medieval sources, and the primitive catacombs betray romanesque affinities. Their architecture is therefore not profoundly in earnest in the familiar Victorian sense but practical, ornamental and associational; only the impressive entrance **14** composition aspires to something more penetrating with those four solemn white Egyptian pylons flanked by evocative miniature temples, but how much of its sheer success is due to Hosking himself is an open question. And why Egyptian anyway? The answer lies amongst the tombs of the Pharaohs whose sombre burial sites had at last yielded to the investigation of European archaeologists in the wake of the Napoleonic campaigns on the Nile. The first attempt to apply Egyptian features to an English building, Peter Frederick Robinson's Egyptian Hall, Piccadilly in 1811, provoked a brief revival of the style in its more purely decorative forms but being impracticable it did not prosper in any consistent way until taken up by the purveyors of the new cemetery movement. For them the awe-inspiring sublimity of the style and its historic associations with life after death rendered it particularly appropriate to the art of funerary design. But it was left to the American founder of Mount Auburn Cemetery, Jacob Bigelow, to use it first in this way on an architectonic scale; there a massively picturesque gateway flanked by lodges and obelisks, dating from 1831, must surely have provided the main precedent for the Abney Park arrangement.

Hosking's original design of 1839 for the entrance gates and lodges, a much more elaborate and decorative affair than that eventually carried out, was perhaps fortunately put aside on grounds of economy. For the final perfection of his alternative, much simplified version, he called in the great expert on Egyptian symbolic decoration and hieroglyphics, Joseph Bonomi junior (1796-1878). Bonomi, the son of an architect, was perfectly capable of large-scale compositions on his own account as his neo-Egyptian facade to Temple Mills, Leeds, of 1842 efficiently demonstrates. But he was never in practice as an architect, becoming in 1860 Curator of the Soane Museum in Lincoln's Inn Fields, an appointment highly suited to his archaeological temperament. What he brought to Hosking's scheme was above all the refinement and learning that the engineer most lacked: apart from general advice on detail and proportion he contributed designs for the winged orbs emblematic of eternal life as well as their attendant hieroglyphic legends which translate as 'The Gates of the Abode of the Mortal Part of Man'. These carved symbols and inscriptions are to be found in the coved cornices surmounting the two lodges, but it is impossible not to trace Bonomi's hand too in the finely incised lotus
22 flower and leaf motifs enriching the upper coving of the gate pylons. The lotus flower reappears in the guise of finials to the cast ironwork of the main gates and to the lower order of the grand palisade which connects them up with north and south lodges. Between them, archaeologist and engineer produced a splendid scenic display, unique in its time, which is by far the most convincing piece of architecture attached to the cemetery. Set back in a spacious forecourt, the whole composition, as it was built in 1839-40, runs to the length of one hundred and eighteen feet and rests throughout on a low plinth of fine-grained Dartmoor granite, pale grey in colour. At the centre and climax four massive free-standing gate pylons, equally seventeen feet high, are constructed of huge solid blocks of white Portland freestone jointed with the utmost precision to show off their monumental boldness. At each

15 Second design for the Chapel 1839, lithograph by J R Jobbins for Collison's Cemetery Interment.

extremity the lodges, north for the cemetery keeper's residence and south for the cemetery company's local office, form symmetrical wings in the shape of little temples with strongly entasised outer angles and deeply coved cornices; above the square granite plinth they are basically of yellow stock brick but faced in gleaming white Portland stone ashlar. The mason contractors for all this work were Messrs Malcott and Son of Newgate Street, City, while Messrs J Hervey and Company of Thames Foundry were responsible for casting the railings and gates.

For the chapel, Hosking at first devised an elaborate gothic double-cell plan arranged symmetrically on either side of an arched carriage entrance in the form of a transept, all surmounted by a central tower and spire. Such a plan would have accommodated separate compartments for the Church of England and for nonconformists, besides also including a scheme for extensive catacombs below ground. It would seem, alas, that the directors had neglected to brief their architect precisely in accord with the Company's intentions because the design was immediately rejected on three counts. In the first place, it was too ambitious and so beyond the shareholders' limited resources; secondly, it was considered more desirable to unite all the religious denominations under one roof as a demonstration of true catholicity, and lastly, the directors equated catacomb burial with elitism and wished to discourage it by providing as little accommodation as was compatible with their business interests. However, two features they enthusiastically approved of were the covered carriage entrance and the prominent central steeple which, they requested, should be incorporated into the new design. As a result of these criticisms, Hosking detached the catacomb scheme from

13 the chapel altogether and made a separate low structure of it a short distance southward. Because the building of the chapel was delayed by successive reductions in plan, the catacombs were proceeded with first and brought to completion by May 1840. They were housed in a discreetly plain rectangular chamber enclosing a procession of shelved vaults and recesses, a subterranean hall descended into from the north by a narrow flight of steps barred by massive iron gates. Only the flat roof was slightly raised above ground, this being surrounded by a solid parapet topped off with ornamental cast iron open panelling. Internal gloom was contrived by a few clerestory lunettes on the long sides opening out into narrow grilled light-wells, and the sole means of access was through a forbidding romanesque arch of stone sheltering the north door. Upon the roof Hosking placed a temporary shed of light materials which would serve as a mortuary chapel until the permanent building could be made ready.

In accordance with the directors' wishes, the new design for the chapel was made on the basis of a single interdenominational cell, having no features which might be interpreted as bias toward any one of the Christian sects who would use it. Its function as a funerary chapel in any case placed it outside of the normal arrangements for a place of worship and so the main internal emphasis was fixed on the centre where the bier could rest in full view. As the style was to be an adaptation of early English gothic of the thirteenth to fourteenth centuries, perhaps the most appropriate way of achieving this kind of centralised space was by use of a cruciform plan. Hosking therefore made his interior in the form of a Greek cross – that is with all four arms equal in length – and resolved the question of a high steeple by raising it centrally over

15 the crossing of transepts and nave. Externally this strict regularity was not so apparent because the nave, or principal body of the chapel, extended south-ward to provide the desired carriage porch and twin turrets containing stair-cases to the public gallery above; similarly at the northern end an extension of equal height was intended for the vestry with yet another big gallery recessed over it. Despite unanimous approval, the excessive cost of this design led to its further paring-down early in 1840, the most obvious omission being the northern vestry-cum-gallery which was substituted by a low, three-sided

16 apsidal robing room clamped onto the now equal north arm. Otherwise it was mostly the enriched detail which suffered, every feature capable of reduction being radically simplified or in some places entirely wiped out, but it is reasonably true that the harsh discipline of economy saved Hosking's chapel from being over-fussy and gave it the distinction of greater architectural cohesion.

George Collison, whose forebears were native to Beverley, was understandably pleased with the idea of an association, however tenuous, of its splendiferous Minster with the comparatively insignificant chapel of Abney Park Cemetery. His book reveals that the architect sought inspiration for his details in that great medieval fane but it is difficult in the extreme to trace the process in the executed work. Only the four wheel windows in the gable fronts can be said to relate directly to one similar, but infinitely more glorious, in the Minster's south transept and then otherwise the resemblances are merely ghostly. In his suspicion that the central tower and spire must have been **19** borrowed from some old village church, Collison hit nearer the mark, for this pinnacled octagon is yet another, if early, Victorian adaptation of the celebrated fourteenth century steeple of Bloxham in Oxfordshire. Hosking's sources, even if just recognisable, are remote therefore and made remoter still by being translated into the London yellow stock brick which he used in the construction, although most of the detail work and dressings are of wrought Bath stone. Within, the walls were entirely plastered and even the complicated arch profiles were modelled in plaster; yet, despite these rather uncouth details, the interior soared impressively on its four polygonal tower-piers to **17** become enveloped in a shadowy plaster-vaulted ceiling. Perhaps the most intriguing part of the building is the brick-vaulted porte-cochère at the **18** southern end of the nave, open to east and west beneath resolutely round-headed brick archways almost in the manner of Soane. What are these skeletal features, strictly neoclassical in origin, doing in a gothic design apart from the sheerly functional? Even in their earlier version as decoratively moulded **15** romanesque arches they would have been extraordinary, but somehow they contribute nicely to the folly-like character of the principal south front with its ogee hooded entrance arch and quaint pair of embattled octagonal turrets. **29** Discounting all eccentricities of style, the romantic charm of the whole piece is undeniable, and in the final analysis utterly disarming, but its chief asset to the landscape remains of course scenic. The one hundred and twenty foot high steeple, intended as a landmark from all key positions, acts as a magnetic focus **1, 13, 35** to the cemetery's layout.

No other comparable London cemetery turned out so fortunate as Abney Park in the possession of its well grown and stately timber inherited from the predecessor estates, so that the decision to retain as much as possible of the old planting happily allowed existing historic patterns to filter through into the **11, 12** new arrangement. Indeed, the major configurations of mature trees and shrubs clearly dictated the route plan in several instances and continued to

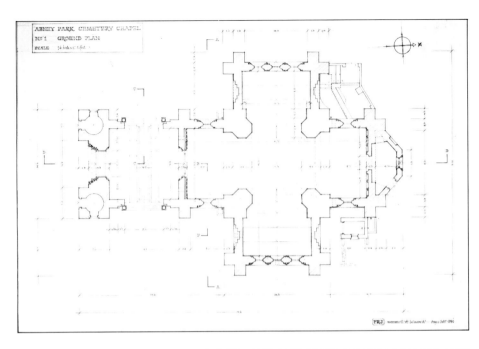

16 Ground plan of the Chapel, from a measured survey by P R Joyce in 1980. The original arrangements included a central bier, with raked floors in the transepts and a large central pulpit in the northern arm of the cross.

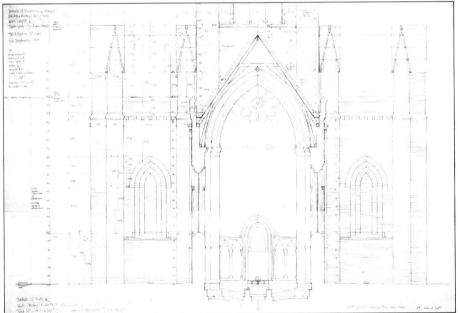

17 Section across the Chapel nave, from the measured survey of 1980.

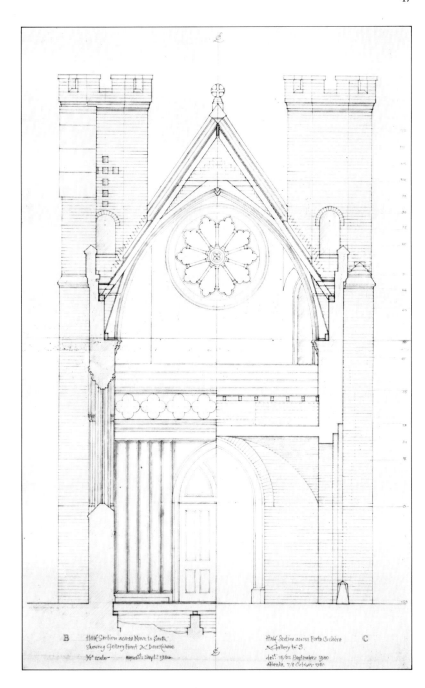

18 Section across the Chapel porch, from the measured survey of 1980. The drawing includes a half section across the nave to show the gallery front and entrance door. Winding wooden staircases in the twin turrets provided access to gallery and roof levels.

19 The Chapel spire

dominate the landscape for many years of the cemetery's early existence. Chief among these, the noble avenues of elms in the northern grounds gave rise to two parallel Elm Walks, the Great and the Little, the latter of which ran **13** northward on the chapel's main axis and was always supposed to have been planted by Isaac Watts. Further afield at the extreme north-east corner, Watts' secluded retreat still lay under the shade of his magnificent horse-chestnut tree, or more likely a direct descendant of it, although a circuit of the same species had to be uprooted for the building of the curved boundary wall. **20** En route from the south, the old long orchard was traversed by paths and replanted in a different way altogether, but Fleetwood's estate also contained various rare seventeenth century importations from the New World such as the tulip tree and American larch which were at that time erroneously thought to have been introduced by the Lieutenant General during the Commonwealth. Strung east to west along the middle of the Fleetwood ground a broad grove of ancient yew trees was converted into the Yew Walk with one end converging with the lower orchard roads. Nearby, further towards the south boundary route, a spectacular feature was made of the great Cedar of Lebanon which, cleared of decayed encroaching wood and dense overgrowth, emerged in prime and healthy state in spite of its estimated one and three-quarter centuries. The tremendous girth of its trunk had gradually absorbed a rusting **8** scythe-blade hung up there and doubtless forgotten many decades before, until in 1840 only the heel end remained barely visible. Other less awe-inspiring cedars were preserved in parts of the grounds, as well as the picturesque groups of tall elms framing Abney Mansion and a fair number of **10** horse-chestnuts.

Merely to base the new planting upon the framework of the old would have resulted in an enlightened piece of conservation but, in line with the original policies of the Abney Park Cemetery Company, the directors had determined on a more ambitious course still. The establishment of an arboretum in connexion with a place of sepulture was so far a quite revolutionary feature not yet taken up by any other comparable British institution, although a similar idea had been put forward as one desiderata of modern cemetery arrangement in Loudon's proposals of 1830. Now Abney Park possessed every qualification possibly required for encouraging the growth of trees. Its virgin soil of the finest character consisted of sufficient varieties of sand, clay and loam intermixed for the planting of appropriate specimens, and it was found that any introduction of foreign soil need be confined only to a few choice American shrubs. Here then was the perfect place to try the experiment, and conveniently near in Hackney existed the most capable nursery for the job.

Commemorated now just by a road name at the north of St Thomas Square, the once celebrated horticultural establishment of Loddiges lay behind Mare

Street in the lush meadows of Paradise Fields, stretching between Paragon and Square eastward to Chatham Place. Its founder, Conrad Loddiges (1738-1826), emigrated in about 1760 from the North German state of Hanover and settled in London as a seed merchant. Having taken over John Busch's nursery near Barber's Barn in Mare Street in 1771, he successively leased new grounds northwards between 1787 and 1792 until some fifteen acres were inclosed. Conrad was a pioneer, responsible for introducing the tribes of rhododendron and dahlia into England but his enterprise also included the novelty of rhubarb; the earliest recorded meal at which it was served in this country took place at a ladies' boarding school in Hackney. As his reputation grew he brought his two sons, William (1776-1849) and George (1786-1846) into a flourishing business, to which they succeeded in 1826. There can be no doubt that George Loddiges was the principal creative genius behind the remarkable botanical developments at Hackney during the first half of the nineteenth century. He pursued wide cultural and scientific interests embracing such diverse subjects as ornithology, microscopic studies and the graphic arts, besides being no mean draughtsman himself. His close association with Joseph Paxton, the landscape gardener and eventual creator of the Crystal Palace, led to the expert construction of the nursery's great curvilinear palm house which, together with its subsidiary temperate houses, sheltered the unrivalled collection of palms, orchids and ferns comprising Loddiges' chief specialities. Camelia and cactus were grown here too among a host of rare tropical plants reported to have been the finest display of exotics yet assembled in England, and from which the Royal Botanical Gardens at Kew drew its supplies. Out of doors, a complete arboretum of hardy trees and shrubs was cultivated.

Between 1817 and 1834 George Loddiges published *The Botanical Cabinet*, its twenty volumes containing two thousand plates beautifully drawn from specimens grown at Hackney. In this work he engaged the talents of his friend George Cooke of Pentonville (1781-1834), son of another anglicised German expatriate and one of the foremost topographical and marine engravers of the day. Cooke became deeply interested in botanical science even to the extent of removing in 1818 with his young family to a house in Loddiges Place, Hackney, where they lived until their departure to Barnes in 1829. His second son and pupil Edward William Cooke (1811-1880) can only be described as a prodigy who, having established and then abandoned a marvellous career in etching between the ages of fifteen and twenty-two, proceeded faultlessly to his lasting fame as a marine painter. But the enthusiasm generated by his father's work at Hackney induced in Edward too a passion for horticulture that, by the sustained encouragement of Loddiges, came almost to be a second profession in landscape gardening. Cooke eventually sealed this intimate

20 Dr Watts' Mound, lithograph from a drawing by G Childs 1840 for Collison's Cemetery Interment.

relationship with the Hackney nursery in 1840 by his marriage to George Loddiges' daughter Jane, although she unhappily died in childbirth in 1843. In view of his increasing involvement in practical landscape design during the later 1830s, it would not be in the least astonishing to discover evidence of Edward William Cooke's influence on the cemetery planting scheme, even if he was not actively concerned in it. Moreover, there is a neat conclusion to be drawn that by their shared Lutheran heritage the Loddiges and the Cookes made themselves particularly amenable to the unconventional outlook of the Abney Park Cemetery Company, although quite apart from such obvious sympathies, none could have been more fit to carry out their arboretum than the nursery of George Loddiges.

Familiar enough to Collison through his nonconformist paternal connexions, it is tempting to identify the indefatigable Registrar with the idea of introducing Loddiges. It is due to him alone that details of the extensive arboretum of Abney Park have survived for he took care to include the entire catalogue of plants in his 1840 publication. The scheme, devised in 1839, embraced all specimens of trees and shrubs sufficiently hardy to bear the English climate and consisted of some 2,500 varieties including a choice

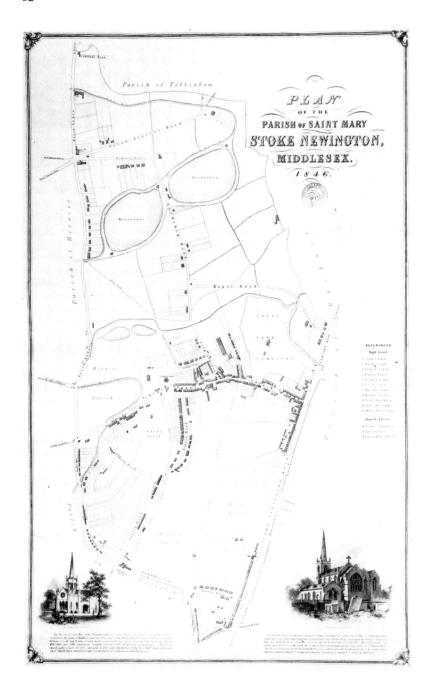

21 **Map of Stoke Newington in 1846**, engraved by Charles Miller with vignettes of the Parish Church of St Mary and the new Chapel of Abney Park Cemetery. Thomas Maughan's development of Listria Lodge and Shaftesbury Villas on the old Ten Acre Field has begun, but apart from the cemetery and Thomas Cubitt's recent creation of Albion Road the greatest physical impact on the district is the appearance of the New River reservoirs constructed in 1830-33.

collection of pines, firs and flowering fruit trees. In addition to this, between three and four acres of the grounds were set aside as a rosarium wherein 1,029 varieties of rose could be cultivated, and later a large selection of American shrubs, magnolia and rhododendron were due to be arranged in clumps near the chapel. Hardy deciduous trees proliferated with a familiar litany of species: ash, oak, beech, willow, elder, poplar, birch, walnut, plane, alder and so on. Less common choices were the quince tree, maple, acacia, wild olive, and the service tree, together with laburnum, dogwood and box. The sadly ephemeral nature of horticultural display makes it impossible now to visualise the original glory of Abney Park as it emerged in the spring of 1840, and to make matters worse, no precise idea of the new planting distribution is available in spite of the splendid lithographic panorama issued just before **13** work was completed. Four other provocative views of the grounds included in **8, 10** Collison's book convey something at least of the resplendent beauty created in **14, 20** this first truly Victorian garden cemetery.

Nearly fifteen hundred people congregated in a marquee for the ceremonial opening and dedication of Abney Park Cemetery on 20 May 1840. On the same occasion, the foundation stone of the chapel was laid by Sir Chapman Marshall, Lord Mayor of the City of London, its brass inscription recording the name of the architect, and also of the builder John Jay of London Wall. Prayers were offered by the two chaplains appointed to the cemetery, the Rev J Kershaw for the Church of England, and the Rev John Jefferson of Abney Chapel for the nonconformist parties. Between these an appropriate oration in praise of cemetery interment was delivered by the Rev Thomas Archer, minister of the Oxendon Street Secession Church in Westminster. Fourteen days later on 3 June business commenced with the funeral of the Rev James Mather of Upper Clapton, whose grave lies in an oddly inconspicuous path some way north of the chapel. It was a characteristic inauguration for the new Campo Santo of Congregationalism which swiftly established its claim as a place of pilgrimage and instructive retreat. The Company prospered from the start, recording more than 5,000 burials in the first decade, rising to nearly 9,000 for the five years 1850-55. Between the latter date and 1875 a peak of over 2,000 interments per year was maintained before levelling off to a measurably lower average. There was at first no orderly infill of grave plots but a somewhat haphazard progress accrued according to the individual caprice of purchasers. In the case of common graves the situation was rather different in that these were relegated to the fringes, sandwiched between main boundary routes and **12** inclosure walls. They threatened to fill so quickly that in about 1860 when Hackney Brook was submerged and culverted as a sewer, the cemetery boundaries were extended over it and their walls rebuilt further out. **70**

J C Loudon, who made his own pilgrimage to Abney Park before 1843, reported favourably on its architecture and monuments but in particular on its planting as 'the most highly ornamented cemetery in the neighbourhood of London'. He observed too with approval that in the summer season such flowers as dahlias, geraniums, fuschias, verbenas and petunias were being planted out in patches. As to the superb arboretum, all the trees and shrubs were named for the interest and instruction of visitors, including the numerous parties of children who were taken for walks within the walls. The enormous value of the plants prevented the grounds from being kept open indiscriminately but respectable applicants were always able to obtain a viewing order. For a time Abney House, as it had finally come to be known, remained an object of intense curiosity on account of its tangible relics of Watts but after three years of occupation its fate was sealed by the departure of the Wesleyan College to new premises. Left to the gaze of visitors for some months, its obituary portraits were commissioned in July 1843 from the topographical artist Thomas Hosmer Shepherd (1793-1864); then shortly after the auction of its component parts, conducted on the premises by Luntley of Shoreditch on 26 July, the house-breakers moved in and reduced Gunston's palace to dust. Fortunately the ornamental iron gate and railings to Church Street were allowed to remain as a secondary entrance. Thrown open to the grounds, the Mansion site became absorbed into the boundary route system and it was planted by Loddiges during the autumn of 1843 as his last substantial operation at Abney Park.

A scheme for the permanent commemoration of Dr Watts by public subscription had been contrived by George Collison as early as 1840. To this end he obtained from the sculptor, James Nixon, an elaborate design for a tall cenotaph surmounted by a statue and included it as the frontispiece to his book. In order to facilitate its erection in the cemetery he offered to purchase a piece of ground out of his royalties, but possibly response was discouraging as nothing came of Nixon's drawing. A fresh opportunity to revive the project was provided by the demolition of Abney House and involved the development of a new walk on its northern axis towards the chapel. Here in Dr Watts' Walk, forward of the catacombs, was placed an idealised stone effigy of the little hymnwriter, bible clasped to breast, gazing towards the airy space where his last home stood. Completed in 1845 it ranks as one of the noblest works of Edward Hodges Baily RA (1788-1867), a prolific sculptor of European reputation trained in Flaxman's studio, and whose most prominent public monument is hoisted aloft on Nelson's Column.

There is no record either of Hosking's or the Loddiges' involvement in subsequent works at Abney Park, although successive maps reveal that a gradual development of the subsidiary road and path network took place throughout most of the early period. However, these changes are more noticeable in the later 1850s and early '60s as demand for access to the remoter areas mounted, until in 1870 the system reached its final form when the **70** imposing avenue of New Road was opened up. But by the commencement of 1850 both Loddiges brothers were dead and deposited in the family tomb on the north side of St John at Hackney Churchyard. Their successor Conrad Loddiges (1821-1865), George's son, allowed the nursery to decline and submit to the increasingly polluted atmosphere of the suburbs so that when the ground leases began to fall in, he sold the remaining stock to the Crystal Palace Company in Sydenham. It was installed there by Sir Joseph Paxton in 1854. As to William Hosking, his later career seems to have evolved out of the disciplines of his professorship at King's College and he became best known as an authority on building regulations. Notwithstanding his very considerable contribution towards the success of Abney Park, the architect chose to be buried in the Hosking family tomb at Highgate Cemetery. There over his grave he had earlier devised an ingenious piece of stonemasonry replete with inscribed instructions on its method of dismantling for future interments.

The first reorganisation of the Company occurred in 1866 by which time all but two of the founding trustees had died. Nine new trustees were appointed in their place but none was of such interest as Charles Reed of Homerton (1819-1881), son of the Congregationalist philanthropist, Dr Andrew Reed. A typefounder and antiquary, he was successively elected the first MP for Hackney and then Chairman of the new School Board for London. He also took the Chair of the Preservation Committee for Bunhill Fields which guided the City Corporation's far-sighted act of conservation in retrieving the old burial ground as a public garden. Subsequently knighted, Reed continued to concern himself in the affairs of Abney Park both as a trustee and director until his death on 25 March 1881. He was probably responsible for guiding the members of the Company towards their incorporation of limited liability registered at the Stock Exchange on 19 March 1881, although the four trustees who survived him did not finally make over the property to Abney Park Cemetery Company Limited until 11 April 1882. Foreseeing an imminent shortage of new burial plots in Abney Park, the reformed Company lost no time in expanding its activities and soon established a new cemetery at Chingford Mount, 1883-84, where the nonconformist tradition might continue unhampered. They later founded other new and superbly planted garden cemeteries at Hendon Park, 1899, and at Greenford Park, after the turn of the century.

22 Egyptian pylons of the entrance gates

A Guide through Abney Park
landscape and memorials

There is a land of pure delight
Where saints immortal reign;
Infinite day excludes the night,
And pleasures banish pain.

There everlasting spring abides,
And never-withering flowers:
Death, like a narrow sea, divides
This heavenly land from ours.

Isaac Watts 1706

No other English cemetery has been better served in its literature than Abney Park. That this was in good measure due to its inherent secondary role as a place of nonconformist pilgrimage is made quite clear by, among other things, the consistency of allusions to Watts, Fleetwood and the Abneys. George Collison's book of 1840 gives them a special pride of place and is, moreover, the most historically reliable account of the cemetery's beginnings available up to the present time. But the guide published in 1869 by the Company's second nonconformist chaplain, Thomas Barker, is primarily a reflection of the once maligned Victorian virtue of sentiment. Unconsciously perhaps, it has the persuasiveness of a deft piece of commercial promotion; its tone is evangelical and utterly sincere, but plays rather too sanctimoniously on a carefully cultivated popular attitude to the paraphernalia of death and burial. In terms that are sweetly consolatory and often more than a trifle cloying, its author conveys a vivid impression of the idyllic necropolis of Abney Park in its first full maturity.

It is as well to remember that at the time Barker was writing no less than 45,000 interments had already taken place in the grounds, a vast array of monuments and gravestones was accumulating, and the special character of the cemetery had recognisably established itself. From his picturesque descriptions, a satisfyingly large number of early memorials may still be identified although, inevitably, some among those mentioned have now entirely disappeared or lie in ruin from neglect and decay. In distinct contrast to the more fashionable of the early public cemeteries of London such as Kensal Green or Norwood, and without doubt partly the result of a deeply ingrained nonconformist habit of thrift, the monuments of Abney Park have mainly acquiesced in a tradition of modesty. In this they take heed of the precedent of Bunhill Fields. There is only one real mausoleum to be found in the whole thirty-one acres, and discounting the entrance composition and the chapel it is the planting which practically always dominates the landscape. From almost any point of view the scale seems intimate, the character romantically sylvan, so that the monuments, many of them of high quality and great variety in design, cannot be considered apart from their proper setting.

By the 1850s several leading monumental stonemasons had strategically encamped themselves in yards near the High Street entrance. Four such firms are particularly worthy of mention: Henry Dunkley, Millward and Company, John Cusworth and Sons, and Messrs Winters and Calip. They are all well represented in the cemetery and often identified their work by a signature in some discreet but visible position on pedestal or kerbstone. Funerary masons like these were able to turn out the whole range of monumental sculpture from the simplest grave-slab or headstone to the most elaborate piece of architectural pomp, although it is not clear how much they were personally responsible for their design. A wide selection of plain and shaped headstones, chest tombs, ledger tombs, high pedestals with plain or draped urns, broken columns raised on pedestals, obelisks likewise, gothic pinnacles also likewise, and a host of other popular forms were basically common to each firm and only varied according to the fancy and skill of the craftsmen involved. Even in cases outside the usual categories the names of the designers remain disappointingly fugitive, few only having so far yielded themselves. Amongst those that have been discovered, the architects Alfred Waterhouse, William Gillbee Habershon, Enoch Bassett Keeling, and Samuel Robinson are of national standing; so too are the sculptors E H Baily and James Forsyth. But many of the finest tomb designs are completely anonymous, beginning with the neo-Grec sarcophagus of James Mather, the first to be interred in Abney Park Cemetery in 1840, right through to the subtle Arts and Crafts sculpture to Harriet Delph in 1946. Somewhere between these fine pieces, conventional white marble angels like those in the New Road inaugurate a less appealing phase of popular funerary art towards the latter years of the nineteenth century; their coldly dramatic poses in combination with a particular brand of sentimental realism betray all too readily the fact that they were imported in droves from Italy.

By the middle of the 1880s indeed in almost all respects Abney Park had embarked upon its long century of decline and erosion. To begin with there

23 The King column in the
entrance drive

24 Monument to Alderman
George Briggs

was a marked drop in the number of burials which cannot be entirely accounted for by the so-called crematorium crisis of 1885, nor by the opening of Chingford Mount Cemetery in the previous year; the figures had already started falling off from their peak of over 2,000 per annum and this alarming symptom was probably the chief factor in the move to reform the Company in 1881. It had to be acknowledged that the cemetery possessed limited capacity for new burials and that space would eventually run out. Nonetheless, interments proceeded at a reduced rate averaging over 1,500 yearly until the second world war, so that by the end of the nineteenth century more than 100,000 burials had been registered and by 1930 about half of that number again. Still at first the old ideals of the Company had not been completely forgotten as brave efforts were made to stay the process of ruin, even to reverse it, particularly in the 1890s when a massive replanting programme was initiated. Of the early timber, the ancient elms were the first victims as they had commenced their slow decay soon after the original drainage works had taken full effect. They were mostly replaced with Lombardy poplars; the yews were replaced by black poplars. In the event all this seems now to have provided only short-term respite as both species, although highly ornamental and appropriate to the landscape, are fast-growing and therefore relatively short-lived. The peripheral shrubberies around the southern boundaries were several times reduced, then successively squeezed out altogether for extra common graves. The 1890s also witnessed the sealing up of the old Church Street gate and the infilling of its entrance drive.

After 1900, in hand with the general replanting work, many new grave plots were devised by the simple expedient of infilling between existing ones so that by extension of this policy much of the spacious botanical garden character of the cemetery was doomed. Eventually the venerable Cedar of Lebanon failed too and was removed by 1920 when its site began to be snapped up for new burials; at the same time wholesale re-use of old plots seems to have been initiated in certain parts of the grounds and an air of general neglect settled over the place. Following up complaints in 1928 the Ministry of Health carried out an investigation into burial conditions as well as criticising the untidy state of the cemetery, and although the Company carried out improvements they received further adverse publicity less than a decade later. Allegations of gross overcrowding of graves, together with the unrestricted use and re-use of ground appeared in the press during 1937: at this late date the same average number of interments was still being maintained every year. Surely Abney Park was as full as it could decently be, yet there is no indication of any forthcoming reform even then. Further degradation came with the 1939-45 war when a high-explosive bomb dropped immediately east of the Abney House site, blowing up several very solid monuments and scattering their huge debris over an astonishingly wide area. No attempt was ever made to clear up the mess or repair the damage. There was however some post-war work on the chapel which entailed reconstructing **19** the tower parapet in simplified form, shaving off the encircling gablets from the four tower pinnacles, re-rendering the spire, and replacing the spire-finial and four main gable crosses. All of this new work, although structurally necessary, was carried out in a peculiarly brutal manner which has resulted in a distinct coarsening of William Hosking's original detail. On a previous occasion, when the brick construction of the spire had needed re-rendering, the old design was simplified by omission of a series of widely spaced horizontal bands of decoration which Hosking had placed to mark his stabilising courses of stone.

Management of Abney Park went from bad to worse after the 1950s when, in common with other early joint-stock cemeteries still controlled by their respective companies, there was not enough revenue to support more than a vestige of adequate maintenance. In a last ditch stand to wrest profit from a sinking enterprise, certain paths and drives were staked out for mass infill burial; a whole section of the important west boundary route was cut off and so used. Dr Watts' Walk came to be all but obliterated by such treatment up to the early 1970s; a good headway was made even in the Great Elm Walk and the Yew Walk, and in other places crucially sited grass verges were drawn in to the disgraceful sacrifice. The shabby entrance forecourt was cynically turned into a car park. However, nothing of this proved of any real avail to the Abney Park Cemetery Company, which had for some time become absorbed into a complex of holding companies and no longer possessed independent existence. In February 1972 they abandoned all responsibility, withdrew what little superintending staff was left, and mortgaged the property. Just less than three years later they were declared bankrupt, the cemetery being placed under legal charge on 21 November 1974. Nothwithstanding this, unauthorised burials continued for another four years with pathetic consequences for the bereaved, and even the local clergy who were called upon to officiate did not at first appear to realise the gravity of the situation.

Predictably enough, immediate response to the exodus of 1972 came in the form of vandalism. Isolated monuments and gravestones began to be defaced, then broken up or overthrown, but the deserted chapel and long disused catacombs made equally susceptible targets and therefore from the beginning were as mercilessly attacked. Although in the long run the chapel sustained the more grievous harm, becoming gradually and systematically reduced to a state approaching ruin, it was the sacrilegious raiding of the catacomb vaults and scattering of their grisly contents which first provoked measurable public indignation. As in the case of Highgate Cemetery, there were rumours of black magic and other equally unsavoury practices. At a meeting of concerned local residents and grave owners which took place in August 1974, the association known as Save Abney Park Cemetery was brought into being. Although at the time it could hardly have been apparent to the originators, their decision to act was an event of more than local signficance for, closely followed by the well publicised and highly successful Friends of Highgate Cemetery in 1975, SAPC turned out to be in the vanguard of a now rapidly multiplying group of voluntary organisations set up throughout England for the conservation of individual Victorian cemeteries. One of the most urgent tasks of the new association was to investigate the obscure ownership of the property and its legal answerability for the continuous stream of burials still being carried out. When the totally unsatisfactory nature of these became all too obvious, SAPC concentrated efforts on helping to persuade the London Borough of Hackney to take over and maintain Abney Park as a public amenity. Fortunately its potential as a valuable open space was recognised and negotiations for purchase proceeded throughout the middle months of 1978, the local authority assuming practical control from October of that year. Conveyance of the property to Hackney Council, dated 8 January 1979, involved the purely nominal sum of £1.

In close consultation with SAPC since 1979, the Borough Council has been getting on with the long and complex job of rescuing Abney Park from its plight. Through years of neglect the dense overgrowth of vegetation had at last rendered extensive inner sections of the cemetery impassable, but almost everywhere nature ran out of control, intensifying the atmosphere of advanced romantic decay. Vast tracts of tombs became progressively engulfed in tidal waves of ivy, twisting convulvulus and bramble; self-seeded sycamore and common ash saplings proliferated wherever they could obtain a foothold, and perhaps most problematic of all the bamboo-like, almost indestructible Japanese knotweed came to invade every patch of ground left open by the wholesale death of elms. Gloomily picturesque as they undeniably were, the network of narrow pathways had to be cleared in the first instance to recover access to the interior of the grounds, then the most dangerous of the large number of degenerating trees needed to be treated or felled. Others fell of their own accord, especially during high winds, and several of the tallest Lombardy poplars were lost in this way. More recently the whole of the black poplars have been pollarded, so that they at least are able to wax with renewed vigour. On the architectural side, spectacular improvements were achieved during 1980-83 with the restoration and cleaning of the main entrance ensemble and the reinstatement of the derelict, fire-scarred lodges. In conjunction with this **22** work the forecourt has been attractively remodelled and landscaped utilising a variety of good traditional materials to complement the bold Egyptian

25 Martha Walton's angel

architecture beyond; and the old wrought iron gate, high railings and walls in Church Street have been sympathetically restored, the gateway now happily reunited with its long-absent curly overthrow. Hidden stretches of crumbling 9 or collapsed boundary wall have been receiving urgent attention, and during 1983 a positive start was at length made on the eroding structure of the chapel which required entire replacement of its roofs.

With the full backing of Hackney Council, SAPC has undertaken a survey of monuments, commenced in 1980, by which it is hoped not only to record all significant memorials but to set in motion a selective programme for their repair and conservation on the lines of that which has already been accomplished for the Isaac Watts monument. Among other proposals under consideration, improvement schemes for the most important walks which have been disfigured by indiscriminate infill burials will, when implemented, have a highly beneficial impact on the beauty of the landscape. Insofar as it has progressed, Hackney's sensible treatment of Abney Park has been quoted as a model that other custodians of historic cemeteries would do well to follow, but what else of the future? Its original function as a burial ground is rapidly drawing to a close for the simple reason that no new plots are available, and the only interments now taking place are in the limited number of existing family graves which still remain unfilled. Re-use of old plots is not in contemplation. In addition to this, the sheer congestion of gravestones of all ages creates special problems for the very necessary replanting work which will soon require putting into effect if the proper character of the landscape is to be perpetuated. Whether as a place of quiet retreat, a memorial park, nature reserve, repository of funerary art, a botanical garden, genealogical archive, or most desirably a combination of all these things, Abney Park Cemetery will undoubtedly continue to attract its share of the revived habit of cemetery strolling, a pastime much enjoyed by the Victorians and not looked upon by them as in any way morbid or necromantic.

The Itinerary

Such melancholy as any earnest pilgrim to the sepulchre may be inclined to feel is at once dispelled by James Branwhite French in his *Walks in Abney Park*, 1883: 'Death is but a contrivance for gaining more life. A walk in such a place as Abney Park need not, and should not, under ordinary circumstances be a mournful exercise. It may be one of bright and beautiful memories of past lives, as well as of joyous contemplation of their present glory, and of its full completion, when mortality shall be swallowed up of all-abounding LIFE'. An itinerary taking in all of the main routes of the cemetery, as well as the most 70 rewarding of the minor paths, may be leisurely followed in just about two hours commencing at the High Street entrance forecourt. Those intending to embark on a more detailed search should be prepared for extended visits, as a large proportion of the tombs vanish beneath dense undergrowth for long

22 periods of the year and are not easy of access. Before passing into 'The Gates of the Abode of the Mortal Part of Man' the former stonemason's shop of Millward and Company, flanking the south end of the forecourt, is worth a glance. Built *c*1930 when Millward took over Dunkley's premises next door, its up-to-the-minute architectural facing of concrete blocks disrespectfully impinges on, but takes up the theme of, the Egyptian south lodge. At the north end a curious balancing feature is provided by the decorative cast iron railings of a subterranean public convenience erected in 1910. Between these two, what was until recently a dreary waste of oil-stained tarmac has now become transfigured by the adroit use of traditional Yorkstone paving set off with red brickwork paths on either side of a granite sett drive. L-shaped shrub beds of brick, solid ash seating and tough granulated bollards complete the symmetrical approach.

Once through the solemn gates another version of romantic formalism comes into play as the apparent regularity turns by degrees into ever increasing picturesque variety. The broad entrance drive intiates the process with a subtle change of direction, its wide grass verges sparingly studded with dark cypresses against a mixed shrub and tree background. At the far end of the green sward, two isolated classical monuments confront each other across the drive like sentinels. That on the south is one of Abney Park's most familiar

23 landmarks, a graceful white marble column erected to the memory of *Robert Scarborough* and *Ethel Rosa*, two young children of *Robert King*, who died within a fortnight of each other during October 1860. It is a grim reminder of the high incidence of infant mortality which characterised the Victorian age, even among the wealthier middle classes. Opposite, on the north, a pretty neo-Georgian domed pavilion with four columns open to the winds, likewise constructed of white marble, celebrates the distinguished City career of a

24 Cumbrian gentleman's son, *Alderman George Briggs JP* (1848-1925), whose own sons here commemorated carried on the solidly respectable family tradition well into the twentieth century. Passing beyond this nicely contrasted pair a choice must be made from three diversified but equally enticing main avenues. Veering off sharply to the left the south boundary route offers a convenient short-cut to the reopened Church Street gate; then centrally the eye is caught by ranks of elevated angels and other memorials of late-Victorian prosperity which flank the straight vista of New Road; and directly ahead the principal drive marks the way forward to the chapel spire. Flexed below

12 the Fleetwood end of Hackney Brook, whose ancient course dictated the irregular shape of Abney Park's northern boundaries and assuming the

26 Gothic monument to
Sarah Walker

27 Classical monument to
Amelia Ellerm

28 **William Lewis headstone**

practical business of arriving pleasantly at the cemetery's hub, this route, called *ROAD I* on the plan, is the best place to begin an exploration.

That the introductory grass verge on the knib of the road has been given up for new grave plots becomes apparent straight off. And what makes this unfortunate start more difficult to accept is that the fatuous modern masonry can never be reconciled with its surroundings. Once passed, however, the true nature of Abney Park asserts with a dense array of open-air sculpture which, like the Victorian self-confidence it seeks to perpetuate, hardly lets up for a single instant throughout the entire grounds. The planting of Road I is well varied, skirting an immense area of Lombardy and black poplar in the south. Then ash, plane and mature sycamore progress to the occasional fir tree, silver birch and horse-chestnut further in towards the chapel. If few monuments call for special attention on their own account their collective value to the landscape is enormous, and more especially so around the middle section of the route where the planting is also at its most attractive.

Starting from the east the following deserve closer scrutiny: a High Victorian gothic headstone with foliated cross disc, to *John Johnson* (1820-1879) **68d** Chief Inspector of the Gas Light and Coke Company, N/J10. The peculiarly hybrid ringed granite column and urn, set on a domed pedestal with gothic **2** corner finials, to *Walter William Milburn Ball* (1891-1893), S/I10. *David John Wade* (1857-1882), an unknown sculptor whose refined portrait medallion is **68a** delicately, and anonymously, carved in granite, N/I9. *Samuel Robinson* (1751-1833), architect; panelled gothic chest tomb imported from Robinson's Retreat **62** in Hackney 1901; and *Martha Walton* of Islington (1811-1874), dentist; white marble pedestal surmounted by a sweet-tempered angel almost entirely over- **25** run by ivy, both S/I9. Slightly northward in *PATH G* is one of an excellent series of well-lettered early headstones displaying carved symbolic vignettes in classical tradition, *Agnes Susan Pesman* (1824-1857); hers depicts a kneeling **68b** female mourner at a tomb and is from Dunkley's workshop, E/H8. Returning to the west corner, *Thomas Anderson Vooght* (1927-1935) has a monumental curved white headstone by J Roberts and Co in the new stripped classicism inspired by Lutyens' Cenotaph design for Whitehall, N/H8. Opposite Path G one of the most rewarding groups in Abney Park commences with the four-square urn-capped monument to *Samuel Bateman* (1772-1845). This and some of its impressive companion pieces, *Henry Valentine Orfeur* (1799-1863) with **59** vivid sea picture, the Puginian gothic *Sarah Walker* (1798-1847), and graceful **26** broken column, signifying a life cut short, to *Amelia Ellerm* (1830-1855) are **27** described in the Select List, but the intrepid student should also explore the fifth rank behind for the remarkable double-faced Celtic-romanesque head-stone to *William Lewis* of Hackney (1807-1881). It is of bold cross disc type with **28** almost indecipherable stylised letters, but the reverse carries an incised geometrical design of great elegance; all S/I8. Recessed beneath the branches of a horse-chestnut *John Swan* (1787-1869), marine engineer, is commemorated

63 by a perfectly normal funerary urn, but the faintly embittered epitaph composed by his daughter sets out to inform posterity that his inventive genius went largely unrecognised, N/H8. *John Homes* of Spitalfields (1779-1860) has a prominent white chest tomb with consoles, a mannerist device more in fashion among the elite of Dr Watts' Walk than here, N/H7. Beyond the crossing of Roads B and C the final lap of Road I is decisively over-shadowed by the castellated turrets and carriage porch of the chapel straight ahead, and so it is easy to miss the granite column of *Henry Dunkley* (1817-1900), monumental stonemason, whose artefacts are scattered far and wide throughout the cemetery, S/17.

By a potent combination of neglect and vandalism the chapel has survived only as an empty shell, although it is scheduled to undergo major structural repairs. Its future use, however, has yet to be formulated. In front of the chapel a funnel-shaped lawn, formerly planted with ornamental shrubs, leads straight across to the north-facing catacombs but in spite of the central position it has managed to attract little out of the ordinary in its flanking monuments. Perhaps the single exception is *Julianna Simon* (1816-1861) with pleasing small-scale sculpture by Cusworth: a female mourner seated by a tomb upon which the inverted torch is an antique symbol of life extinguished, E/I6. Shortly after 1922 the low catacomb vaults were externally transformed into a *War Memorial* for servicemen buried in various parts of the grounds without individual inscriptions. The long metal roll-call mounted on the rear wall was amplified after the second world war. In front of this the catacombs roof is laid out with a formal shrub bed and parapet walk reached by steps either side of the original entrance arch. It makes a well elevated setting for the Great War Cross, designed by the architect Sir Reginald Blomfield (1856-1942) for the Imperial War Graves Commission in 1919, of which some forty examples were subsequently erected in various parts of England. From this

29 platform there is a spectacular view of the chapel and its surrounding tall vegetation.

The axis upon which both chapel and catacombs are based forms the spine of Abney Park's layout. It is taken southward to the site of Abney House as *DR WATTS' WALK*, the cemetery's holy of holies. Although not marked on the

1 earliest plan, this walk became established by 1845 when Baily's statue of *Isaac Watts DD* (1674-1748) was placed at its head and it soon attracted the most prestigious clients. Close planted and narrow, its umbrageous grove of silver birches has been marred by disorderly infill burial, much of which is mercifully capable of being mitigated. Greensward around Watts' statue was despoiled too with unsympathetic modern gravestones, but the atmosphere of

29 South view of the Chapel
from the War Memorial

the walk miraculously survives the onslaught due to the strong character of its phalanx of chest tombs and obelisks. Close by the Watts monument in *STATUE PATH B* an Edwardian baroque triumphal arch to the murdered **66** Police Constable *William Frederick Tyler* (1877-1909) should be sought first, N/K6. Then proceeding south from the statue: the impervious Aberdeen granite obelisk of *William Leavers* of Surbiton (1792-1867) towers over the **30** lovely urn-crowned chest tomb of *John Beazley* (1790-1851) nearby, both E/K6, **67** and forces comparison with a strange blunt obelisk to *Rev Algernon Wells* (1793-1850) opposite, W/K6, whose design speaks emphatically the last word in stripped neoclassicism. *Margaret Ord Whipple* (1787-1846) has a serene **31** female figure-sculpture standing, cross in hand, on a rather thin pedestal from which all inscriptions have vanished. The chilling contrast between this and **51** its next-door neighbours, weird twin obelisks erected in 1850 by the brothers *Andrew* and *John Hart*, comes with something of a jolt, all E/L6. Harts',

30 The Beazley tomb in Dr Watts' Walk

31 Monument to Margaret
Ord Whipple

together with most of the following monuments, are given in greater detail in the Select List: *Dr John Pye Smith* (1774-1851), a plain pedimented chest tomb; *Rev Thomas Lewis* (1772-1852), a consoled mannerist chest tomb, and a simplified version to *Rev John Yockney* (1790-1852), all E/L6. Across the way is

53 the sensuous Italianate sarcophagus of mason-contractor *John Jay* (1805-1872) erected for his son in 1853-54, W/L6. *Henry Thomas* of Islington (1815-1853) has a fluted broken column of good proportions which groups nicely with the adjacent mixed-style funerary urn of *Rev John Mason* (1781-1864), both E/L6. Horticulturalist *Conrad Loddiges* (1821-1865) and his wife *Susanna Agar née Bowes* (1819-1897) are buried together in the Bowes family vault, W/L6. The important tombs of *Dr John Harris* (1802-1856) and *Samuel Morley MP* (1809-1886) have, at the time of writing, become swallowed up in an explosion of Japanese knotweed, a fate similarly shared by *Reuben Wakefield* of City Road (1789-1858) whose concave-sided granite monument by W and J Freeman of Penryn offers an idiosyncratic variation on the obelisk theme, all W/M6. The totally unostentatious chest tomb of *Rev John Clayton* (1754-1843) was brought here from Bunhill Fields; another more costly chest tomb, *Dr Thomas Aveling* (1815-1884) is next to it, both E/M6. Then come *Thomas Merriman Coombs* (1790-1863), one of the cemetery's founders, and *Dr Henry Forster Burder* (1783-1864), both W/M6; *Samuel Sharpe* (1799-1881) the Egyptologist, E/M6;

45c and finally at the southernmost point *William Dennis* (1787-1886) a Director of the Abney Park Cemetery Company, S/M6.

On either side of the Dennis urn Dr Watts' Walk splits into two diverging paths to form a triangle with the Abney House site. Westward, *BRANCH B* was made virtually impassable by wholesale infill but contains a plain pedestal monument to *James Braidwood* (1800-1861), the enterprising London Fire Chief killed in the Tooley Street holocaust, W/N6. On the other hand *BRANCH A*, while also suffering some infill, remained passable but was left intolerably narrow by the incongruously sited *Municipal War Memorial*, E/N6. Erected by the former Metropolitan Borough of Stoke Newington after the second world war it commemorates some of the local civilian casualties of the blitz, and is deserving of a better position. Of the 122 deaths recorded here no less than 97 are associated with the disaster at Coronation Avenue flats on 13 October 1940 when a direct hit burst gas and water mains which inundated an air raid shelter. All those taking refuge within, many of them Jewish, were killed.

The two branches of Dr Watts' Walk emerge at either end of *ROAD E*, a short but historically important avenue running along what was formerly the terrace and garden front of Abney Mansion. Its light planting consists mainly of silver birches but the eastern part became desolate and strewn with broken masonry due to the effects of a bomb during the second war. Then afterwards, unscrupulous and improperly carried out infill in the centre of the walk completed the grim scene in this once highly regarded enclave. On the north side are buried several eminent nonconformist divines including *Rev Thomas Boaz* (1806-1861), *Dr John Campbell* (1795-1867), and *Rev Nun Morgan Harry* (1800-1842) but their tombstones are decayed beyond recognition. Remaining complete are the tough neoclassical headstone to *Dr Robert Philip* (1791-1858) and marble pedestal of *Dr John Morison* (1791-1859), but rising above all, against the luxurious textures of a tall old swamp cypress, the noble granite cross in memory of 'The Children's Friend', *Dr Alexander Fletcher* of Finsbury **49** Chapel (1787-1860), all N/N6. The central feature of the south side is a slim red granite obelisk to the relentlessly philanthropic *Dr Andrew Reed* (1787-1862); he obtained a place for his last rest where earlier stood the garden threshold of the great house. Next to him is *Rev William Ellis* (1804-1872) the South Seas missionary, both S/N6, but practically all else as far as the easternmost point remained a detective's puzzle until the rescue work of 1987-88.

32 Abney House Corner and Dr Rogers' mausoleum

33 Gothic shrine of Henry Richard MP

32   As its name implies *ABNEY HOUSE CORNER* curves round the southern edge of the mansion site to link up the main boundary routes. Formed in 1843 after the demolition of the house it was for twenty years kept free of interments as part of a new ornamental layout connected with the Church Street entrance. Dr Rogers' family mausoleum was first to break this embargo and it did so spectacularly, remaining isolated in its central position until both sides of the road began gradually to be taken up in the 1870s. By the end of the century demand was so pressing that the entrance gate was sealed and the old drive given over to infill burial; now access to the recently reopened gate is by a narrow footway through the tombs. Apart from the ubiquitous sycamore and one or two specimens of decorative evergreen the older vegetation here has become abjectly sparse and so cannot compete with the monuments, several of them among the most imposing in the cemetery. Proceeding from east to west: an obelisk shattered by bomb blast rises above the tomb of *Sir Charles Reed* (1819-1881), Hackney's first MP, N/N6; *Rev Edwin Paxton Hood* (1820-1885), an obelisk to *Dr Thomas Binney* (1798-1874) the so-called Archbishop of Nonconformity, both S/N7, and the Rock of Ages for *Dr Alexander Raleigh* (1817-1880), S/O7, follow in close succession and confirm the intention of this quarter as the Congregationalists' Valhalla. Then the magnificent Kilkenny
60 high cross to *Andrew Holmes Reed* (1848-1892) and his brother *Talbot Baines*

Reed (1852-1893), N/O6; the arcaded gothic shrine of *Henry Richard MP* (1812- **33** 1888), the Apostle of Peace, S/O6; and most ambitious of all *Dr Nathaniel Rogers* (1808-1884) whose gleaming marble house tomb reveals a determination **32** to rest in the style to which he had become accustomed, N/06. Beyond this classical eye-catcher are the trimly tended grave plots of *Catherine* (1829-1890) **46** and *General William Booth* (1829-1912), N/O6; also *William Bramwell Booth* (1856-1929), S/O6, and other early heroes of the Salvation Army. Further round *Evelyn Pyle* (1844-1893) daughter of the second Conrad Loddiges, N/O6, and a nicely diversified group of big Victorian and Edwardian monuments turns the corner into Road E. Later, a proliferation of tall Italianate marble angels grew out of the long space behind.

Abney House Corner runs without pause into *ROAD B*, here called the *WEST BOUNDARY ROAD*, whose southern section contains two memorials of great interest: the Celtic cross of *Dr Henry Allon* (1818-1892) minister at the celebrated Union Chapel, Islington; and the elegant Arts and Crafts deadboard of architect *Joseph Douglass Mathews* (1838-1923); both E/M5. From its **55** junction with Road G the west boundary route has been cut off for a considerable length by modern infill burials and is very difficult of access because of rampant overgrowth. However, there are no monuments of outstanding importance in this part. At the beginning of *ROAD G* lies the hipped coffin **35**

34 Minnie Blackwell's Masonic epitaph

35 A group of tombs in Road G

78

tomb of *Dr Robert Halley* (1796-1876), E/L5, and further north by towering Lombardy poplars Statue Path B opens briefly a mysterious apparition of the Watts monument within its wooded hinterland. Northward again the sharp convergence of *ROAD F* and Catacomb Walk presents a varied cluster of tombs
47 including the massive somnolent lion of *Frank Bostock* (1866-1912), and round-
34 topped headstone of *Minnie Blackwell* (1893-1949) with wreathed Masonic symbol carved above bold letters, both N/J5. It is worth making a short diversion into *CATACOMB WALK* to compare another contemporary headstone by the same firm, Winters of Stoke Newington, for *Percy David Desborough* (1906-1943), N/J5. The restrained outline and finely controlled
36 inscription are an object lesson to present day funerary masons.

From the top of Road G the entry into *GREAT ELM WALK* still impresses extremely although, alas, the immemorial elms have long since vanished. Instead this broad and ancient avenue now proceeds between tall Lombardy poplars and a magnificent line of horse-chestnuts, but inevitably the blight of infill has eaten into its best stretch. Tombs are on the whole of secondary
37 interest here; nonetheless a handful should be sought out: *Clara Louisa Brown* (1855-1912), a crisp adaptation of the antique granite Cornish cross; *Emil Schüll* (1830-1854), seemingly conventional neo-Grec with low pediments and bolted marble panels – the inscriptions in German – but its structure is metal-framed with artificial stone cladding; both W/H5. At the corner of Path K another oddity, *James Cook* (born and died 1845), has a slim stone pier with draped cornice whose amorphous topknot eventually resolves itself into a coronet, E/E5. After this it is most convenient to take the excursion into *PATH T* for *Henry Vincent* (1813-1878), a leading figure in the Chartist movement, S/E4. His family headstone is almost frugally sober, a disappointment more than adequately redressed by the wonderful scrolly pedimented headstone to
56 *Lancelot James Mayer* (1819-1849) opposite, N/E4; an expressive pointing hand bids us read the inscription. In remoter regions of Path T gothic family tombs of *Sir Edward Henry Sieveking* (1816-1904) huddle beside an impenetrable thicket of varied oaks, N/E3. Returning to Great Elm Walk: *Mary Bromley Wand* (1823-1846) has a decorously carved headstone illustrating an urn veiled by weeping willow, E/D5, and just by Path Q stands the monumental
61 head-stone to *Ann Rippen* (1810-1849) with exquisite grief-laden medallion sculpture, W/D5. At its north end the broad walk divides in two, the sharp point being occupied by an upright marble slab now but faintly inscribed to *William Thomas* of Shoreditch (1824-1847), N/C5. It is richly finished off with a carved·frieze and deep cornice. Curving away to the left Branch E is entirely blocked by infill, leaving *BRANCH F* to provide exit to the North Boundary Route. Near its top corner a curious hexagonal pillar of red granite, family monument of *Charles Walker Norwood* (1800-1864), is capped with a draped

36 Headstone to Percy David Desborough

37 Cornish cross of Clara Louisa Brown

beehive, W/B5. Other similar monuments to the Norwoods are to be found in Chingford Mount Cemetery and are symbolic of Freemasonry.

Eastward along the North Boundary Road the unassuming entry into *LITTLE ELM WALK* is shortly reached. Opposite, at its head, looms an enormous horse-chestnut but the walk turns out to be surprisingly narrow considering the central status it retains in Abney Park's layout. Apart from the endemic sycamore rash at the north end much of its historic tree cover was wiped out by Dutch elm disease, ideal conditions for an amazing bamboo jungle of Japanese knotweed which has since overwhelmed the middle section. A dearth of interesting memorials is largely made up for by the strange, remote atmosphere but the constant head-on vision of the chapel spire prevents any real sense of disorientation. On the corner of Path K lies *Dr James Bennett* (1774-1862), E/E6, but the thing to see is the Grecian marble sarcophagus of *Rev James Mather* (1775-1840), the earliest tomb in the

38 John Spreat's monument under the Indian bean tree

cemetery, tucked away just inside the western limb of *PATH L*, N/F6.

Below Little Elm Walk, Branches C and D spill out under the black poplars of *CHAPEL LAWN*. Between their two openings a splendidly isolated Indian
38 bean tree shades the tower-like gothic monument to *John Spreat* (1799-1865), an early design by Alfred Waterhouse, architect of Manchester Town Hall and the Natural History Museum at South Kensington, N/G6. Across the lawn
65 presides the solemn marble angel of *Elizabeth Tollady* (1827-1855), E/H6. From the chapel porch an avenue of Lombardy poplars carries the main drive westward as *ROAD H*. Past Great Elm Walk, three highly enriched memorials behind the front ranks will repay the trouble of finding them: firstly the
69 headstone of *Joseph John Newman* has a lunette panel with urn and weeping willow, N/H5; then an urn-capped pedestal by Dunkley for *William Foster* (1824-1860) has an oval vignette with a tree violently struck down by the hand
68c of God, S/I4; and further on the superb headstone of *Emma Elizabeth Wildish* of Hoxton (1824-1858) displays its inscription in a bold rococo cartouche below a carved willow-and-tomb lunette, N/H4. Opposite the entrance to Path P the original memorial to *John Vine Hall* (1774-1860) has been superseded by that of his eminent son *Dr Christopher Newman Hall* of Surrey Chapel (1816-1902). Close by is the chest tomb of his predecessor at Blackfriars, *Rev James Sherman* (1796-1862) one of the founding fathers of Abney Park Cemetery, both S/I3, and facing it the unfussy gothic headstone to *Rev Thomas Toke Lynch* (1818-1871), N/H3. After this the curve of Road H merges imperceptibly into the remaining section of *WEST BOUNDARY ROAD*, a lightly planted grassy drive with few monuments of special note but from which a labyrinth of minor pathways issues in the direction of Great Elm Walk. Within *PATH N* lurks the
40 stylish little monument to *Harriet Delph* (1862-1944), S/G3. Higher up the boundary route is the ledger stone of *Dr John Leifchild* (1780-1862), W/D2, then facing Path U an urn-capped obelisk by Dunkley marks the family tomb of *David Methven* (1818-1867) engineer to the Imperial Gas Works, W/C2.

The route now veers eastward into the intermittent shades of *NORTH BOUNDARY ROAD* with dense clusters of mature ash and sycamore. It becomes ever more evident that in the less cultified northern regions of Abney Park headstones far outweigh any other form of memorial, but their great variety and excellent lettering make them nonetheless worth study. Two quite individual examples belonging to the 1850s stand out beyond the front ranks:
39 *Thomas Marshall* with delicately carved open Bible and palm fronds, and slightly further back *William Hagger* bearing a large wreathed urn relief of a different colour stone from its background, both S/B3. Placed centrally opposite the two branches of Great Elm Walk, a barely legible plain headstone celebrates the phenomenal local character *Mary Hillum* (1759-1864) who died in her 105th year in the same house in which she had been born. It was

39 Symbolic headstones of Thomas Marshall and William Hagger

40 Arts and Crafts sculpture
on Harriet Delph's tomb

**41 High Victorian gothic
monument to Agnes Forsyth**

attached to her baker's shop on the south of Church Street, site of the present Rose and Crown. Despite her longevity Miss Hillum is reputed never to have travelled by omnibus or railway, nor had she ever ventured further than fifteen miles from home, N/B5. Quite exceptional in this part of the grounds is the panelled gothic chest tomb of *Rev William Lockwood Thornton* (1810-1865), S/B6. As the road bends south Path S leads off in deep gloom to the most hidden recess of Abney Park Cemetery, *DR WATTS' MOUND*, long since **20** pitifully derelict and divested of its crowning horse-chestnut tree. A bleak granite tablet remains to tell of its unique history: 'This Mount Was A Favourite Retirement Of The Late Isaac Watts, D.D.' Below in *PATH R* a tall headstone to *Charlotte Larman* (1833-1848) portrays her mourner beside a tomb under weeping willows, E/C8. Even before Path S the eastern arm of the long boundary route, here called *MOUNT ROAD*, had plunged into dark mystery, its tree canopy now taking on a genuine woodland character. Well-lettered early headstones predominate over all other monuments: the grave of *Edward Calvert* (1799-1883), romantic artist and protégé of Blake, is no exception and was by his own choice obscurely enfolded within commonplace plots towards Path R, E/C7. Further south where Lombardy poplars begin, the fallen headstone of young *Charles Dunham Green* (1838-1857) lay in a tangle of undergrowth but has now been re-erected. Beneath its curly pediment an oval vignette has weeping willows framing a broken column, E/G7. The controversial literary satyrist *William Hone* (1780-1842) and his sixth daughter *Rose Hone* (1818-1898), W/H7, present an identical pair of severe neoclassical headstones **52** and opposite, Dunkley's monument for *Amos Tewksbury* (1803-1868), E/H7, **45b** brings the epic Road B to a close with an urn so energetically draped that it almost transmutes into metaphor. The plain oblong pedestal on which it stands rises to intricately carved pediments.

Across the main drive *ROAD C* continues the Lombardy avenue southward, skirting the site of Fleetwood's long orchard between the two old estates. It contains some excellent monuments, including a nice variety of urns, but the **45a** south section has been spoiled by infill. Particularly noteworthy are the massive female figure mourning over the tomb of *Fanny Mechi* (1799-1845), **57** and by its side a pointed headstone with delicate portrait medallion of a youth, **44** *Horace Pickford Kimbell* (1877-1895), both W/J7. At the bottom end a gargantuan slab of granite perpetuates the memory of *Samuel Bagster*, publisher (1772-1851), E/K7, and marks the corner into *YEW WALK*. The old Fleetwood shrubbery is no longer bounded by yews, of course, but has pollarded black poplar and a few remnants of Lombardy. Facing each other at its opening there are well differentiated monuments to *Rev Hezekiah Clement Dukes* of Dalston (1809-1876), N/K7, and to the prolific benefactor *Thomas Wilson* (1764-1843), S/L7, the latter a big chest tomb of extreme sobriety.

Otherwise the only really distinctive piece was a vermiculated tapering mono-lith to *Rev Samuel Martin* (1817-1878), N/K9, now re-erected, and needless to say the avenue is utterly mutilated by infill. Towards its eastern end *PATH E* contains the tombs of *Rev Thomas James* (1789-1873) and the Demarara missionary *Rev Joseph Kelley* (1802-1875), both N/K9, as well as providing a less repetitive approach to the commencement of *ROAD A*.

42 **Tomb of Benjamin Hastie**

The *SOUTH BOUNDARY ROAD*, as it is otherwise named, starts off from King's column with Lombardy poplars but changes over to the black variety on its long curve westward. Not far from the column an appropriately foliaged gothic headstone marks the grave of horticulturalist *James Shirley Hibberd* (1825-1890), E/K10, then a gaunt obelisk to *Abel Simner* (1814-1893) faces the spacious entrance to Yew Walk with hand aloft, confidently indicating the heavens, E/L10. Further into the bend a neat row of austere chest tombs includes one to *William Flanders* of the London Missionary Society (1776-1854),

41 W/M10, and further again a poignant French gothic monument to *Agnes Forsyth* (1861-1864) enshrines the ideal image of Victorian sentiment, N/M10. It is the striking creation of Agnes' father, the sculptor James Forsyth, who was

42 also responsible for the low skeletal tomb of *Benjamin Hastie* (1786-1865) immediately behind in *PATH D*, S/M10. Gothic of quite a different order is

50 present in the richly ornamented headstone to *Catherine Sarah Caroline* (1844-1848), young daughter of architect *William Gillbee Habershon*. It was brought from St Neots in 1852 and placed next to the grave of her grandfather *Matthew Habershon*, architect (1789-1852), N/M10, but his headstone no longer stands. The unremarkable tomb of *Josiah Conder* (1789-1855), author and poet, lies back from Road A in the third rank, N/M9. On the same side *CEDAR PATH* loops round the site of the ancient Cedar of Lebanon which once graced Fleetwood's gardens. The circuit has collected some fine monuments: *Martha Ann Abbott* (1799-1863), a high rectangular pedestal and urn by Cusworth,

back E/L8; the tall broken column of fluted marble to *David McLaren* (1784-1850) by

cover J S Farley of Clerkenwell; and, emphatic in its central position, a dark massive obelisk to *Dr Joseph Fletcher* of Stepney (1784-1843), both N/L8. Just within

58 *PATH B* is the chest tomb of *James Bronterre O'Brien* (1805-1864), a much revered Chartist leader and protagonist for socialism, E/L7; then in *PATH A* the pithy granite column of *Dr Thomas Archer* (1806-1864), and a practically

64 hidden crocketed gothic shrine to *Dr Arthur Tidman* (1792-1868), both N/L7. Road A is quickly regained via the western exit of Cedar Path and terminates without drama at Abney House Corner. Opposite, over the cemetery wall, is the place occupied by Fleetwood House until its demolition in 1872.

From this position *ROAD D* strikes north along the old boundary between Fleetwood and Abney lands. Although heavily infilled throughout and swamped by sycamore saplings it retains much character on its western side;

43 Tomb of Elizabeth Moat

here is perhaps the least demonstrative millionaire's tomb in existence, that of *John Remington Mills* (1798-1879), reticent to the point of inscrutability, W/M6. At the top crossing *STATUE PATH A* burrows through dense wood towards Dr Watts' Walk, passing a Tudor gothic chest tomb inscribed to *Elizabeth Moat* (1786-1846), N/K7; this is decorated with rich panelling and angled corners. **43** Watts' statue guides a sharp transition into the eastern arm of *ROAD F*. Bunyan's biographer *George Offor* (1787-1864) is here, S/K6, facing an opulent arcaded chest tomb to *Alexander Masters Bidgood* (1799-1851), N/J6. The broad, straight walk proceeds over Road C into the grand formality of *NEW ROAD*, an avenue of black poplars giving way to Lombardy towards its eastern end. Many imposing late-Victorian monuments line the route but in general they are not so appealing as their older counterparts. Best of all is the tall gothic pinnacle in memory of *Harriett Elizabeth Cakebread* (1833-1861) dating from the **48** pre-New Road era, then nearby stands a rather dull monument to *Dr George Smith* of Trinity Chapel, Poplar (1803-1870), both N/J7. Comedian *George Leybourne*, better known as 'Champagne Charlie', (1842-1884), and his equally talented son-in-law *Albert Chevalier* (1861-1923), lie in the anonymous ranks behind, N/J8. A little further on the distressingly brief life of *Carrie Hines* (1888-1889) has been commemorated by an enervated version of the Cakebread pinnacle, by Millward, N/J8. Only two other large monuments need be mentioned: a high Celtic cross to *Agnes Agatha Newton* (1842-1900) by Millward, and an inflated gothic headstone resembling a reredos, by Winters, for the family of *Alfred Tallent* (1834-1871), both N/J9. Conspicuously in view ahead, the serene King column brings the itinerary to its conclusion near the main gates.

Time, like an ever rolling stream,
Bears all its sons away;
They fly forgotten, as a dream
Dies at the opening day.

Our God, our help in ages past,
Our hope for years to come;
Be Thou our guard while troubles last,
And our eternal home.

Isaac Watts 1714

44 Medallion portrait of Horace Pickford Kimbell

a

b

45 A group of four funerary urns
a John Brooks Hill in Road C
b Amos Tewkesbury in Mount Road
c William Dennis in Dr Watts' Walk
d Eliza Mary Ward in Path A

c

d

Graves, Tombs and Monuments
a select list

Of those interred in Abney Park Cemetery, the greatest single phenomenon is that galaxy of popular orators and theologians who ranked among the most distinguished metropolitan Congregationalists of the last century. Christian missionaries, social reformers and educationalists are well represented too and form collectively a supporting species in this evangelical hierarchy. Otherwise the most eminent names are those associated with literary, architectural or artistic achievements, as well as the more diverse professions of engineering, medicine and horticulture. All of these urbane activities are reflected in the following selection of over one hundred and thirty tombs, but a number have also been included for their own specific interest as monuments whether it be in excellent design, fine lettering, picturesque grouping or just fanciful eccentricity. Few indeed are attributable to individual designers, although in many cases the stonemasons signed their work and these have been identified in the list. Each entry is followed by the route location together with a grid reference to the plan.

70

ALLON, Rev Dr Henry   1818-1892

Congregationalist divine and hymnologist. Minister of Union Chapel, Compton Terrace, Islington 1852-92 in succession to Rev Thomas Lewis, and was responsible for the ambitious rebuilding programme there between 1874 and 1890 from designs by James Cubitt. Author of a *Memoir of James Sherman*, 1863, and editor of *The British Quarterly Review*, 1866-86. His second son Henry Erskine Allon (1864-1897), also buried here, was a composer.

Grey granite Celtic cross with finely incised surface patterning and bold projecting bosses to the cross head. Possibly designed by James Cubitt c1892.

West Boundary Road B   E/M5

ALTHANS, Andrew Henry   1784-1855

Advocate of popular education and founder of the Abbey Free Schools in East London, Althans was also lay pastor of a small congregation of weavers and artizans in Bethnal Green.

Simple white stone pedestal with practically illegible inscriptions.

Road I   N/H8

ARCHER, Rev Dr Thomas   1806-1864

Pastor of The United Presbyterian Church, Oxendon Street, Westminster 1831-64; a famous orator of great eloquence, he preached at the opening ceremony of Abney Park Cemetery on 20 May 1840.

His monument is a heavily ringed, big polished red granite column in the High Victorian gothic manner, surmounted by a stiff-leaf capital and low octagonal pyramid with finial. Mason: A MacDonald of Aberdeen c1865.

Path A   N/L7

AVELING, Rev Dr Thomas William Baxter   1815-1884

Minister of Kingsland Congregational Chapel, Dalston 1838-84, and Honorary Secretary to the Reedham Home for 37 years. Chairman of the Congregational Union for 1876.

Stone chest tomb with ridged top. Mason: Cusworth c1859.

Dr Watts' Walk   E/M6

BAGSTER, Samuel   1772-1851

Founder of the publishing house of Bagster and Sons, Paternoster Row, City in 1816; specialised in polyglot scriptural and liturgical editions. His eldest son, Samuel Bagster junior (1800-1835), a Baptist, established his own works in 1824 and printed many of the firm's publications. Buried at Tottenham Court Chapel in 1835 his remains were afterwards transferred to Abney Park. The elder Samuel's wife, Eunice, also interred here in 1877, died on the eve of her 99th birthday.

Table tomb with a cyclopean ledger slab of granite supported on bulbous feet, all mounted on a low podium.

Road C   E/K7

BATEMAN, Samuel   1772-1845

'A very old inhabitant of Saint Leonard, Shoreditch' whose large square monument of white stone has Tudor arched inscription panels topped by a low pyramid and sumptuous urn. Mason: Edwin Dunkley c1845.

Road I   S/I8

BEAZLEY, John   1790-1851

Family vault of John and Elizabeth Beazley of Old Ford; a superb baroque chest tomb building up to a central concave-sided pedestal with delicately garlanded urn, c1851.

Dr Watts' Walk   E/K6

BENNETT, Rev Dr James   1774-1862

Congregationalist theologian and author of a *History of Dissenters*; Principal Theological Tutor at Rotherham Independent College 1813-28; pastor of Silver Street Chapel in London 1828-40, and afterwards of the successor chapel in Falcon Square 1842-60. He was father of the physician Sir James Risdon Bennett.

Plain stone chest tomb with ledger top, 1847.

Little Elm Walk   E/E6

BINNEY, Rev Dr Thomas   1798-1874

Congregationalist divine. Pastor of The King's Weigh House Chapel 1827 onwards in succession to the elder John Clayton, and laid the foundation stone of the new chapel in Fish Street Hill near London Bridge in 1834. A popular and erudite preacher, Binney was affectionately known as the Archbishop of Nonconformity.

Tall pink granite obelisk on a low, stepped pedestal. Mason: A MacDonald & Co of Aberdeen 1874.

Abney House Corner   S/N7

BLACKBURN, Rev John   1791-1855

First minister of Claremont Chapel, Pentonville 1819 onwards, and one of the originators of the Congregational Union. First editor of the *Congregational Year Book*. In later life he was led into serious pecuniary difficulties and became ostracised by his co-religionists, although Thomas Binney thought well enough of him to conduct his funeral.

Ironically the tomb has disappeared without trace.

Road H   S/I5

BOAZ, Rev Thomas   1806-1861

Congregationalist missionary in India; pastor of Union Chapel in Calcutta from 1834, and afterwards established a Christian Institute for the youth of India at Bhomanipore.

Monument destroyed.

Road E   N/N6

BONTEMS, John Francis   1814-1888

Of Islington. A Trustee and Director of the Abney Park Cemetery Company from 1866 until its conveyance to the new Limited Company in 1882.

Scrolled tomb slab of polished red granite, c1888.

Abney House Corner   S/O6

BOOTH, William   1829-1912

Founder and first General of the Salvation Army 1878-1912. A Nottingham pawnbroker's assistant of half-Jewish descent, Booth migrated from the Established Church via Chartism to the Methodists before arriving in London in 1849. Through his activities as a lay preacher for the Methodist New Connexion, he met Catherine Mumford of Brixton (1829-1890). They married in 1855. It was a formidable partnership, each supplying what the other lacked; Catherine, a semi-invalid, was a cultured dissenter of rather conventional outlook and William an unlearned enthusiast for revivalism. His reputation for violent methods in the pulpit led to his final break with Methodist authority in 1861 when he launched on his career of independent revivalism. After a period as an itinerant preacher he was persuaded by Mrs Booth to open a Christian mission in Whitechapel 1865. This was resolved into the Salvation Army in 1878. Catherine Booth, no mean orator herself, died of cancer in 1890 and was buried in Abney Park. General Booth's funeral **3** in August 1912 was a spectacular event and drew thousands out onto the streets.

Their grave is marked by a bold Salvation **46** Army shield of blue Pennant sandstone with gilt inscriptions, propped up beyond a sea of crazy paving. Mason: Winters c1912.

Abney House Corner   N/O6

BOOTH, William Bramwell   1856-1929

Second General of the Salvation Army 1912-29. Eldest son and successor of William Booth, Bramwell was the crusading organiser of the Army, becoming Chief of Staff in 1880. His wife Florence née Soper (1861-1957), a Salvationist Commissioner since 1888, is also buried here.

Smaller version of the Salvation Army shield with succinct gilt inscriptions worthy of full quotation –
'W:Bramwell:Booth
General Of The Salvation Army
Born 8th March 1856
Born Of The Spirit 1863
Promoted To Glory 16th June 1929
Servant Of All
And Of His Wife
Florence:E:Booth
Born 12th September 1861
Born Of The Spirit 5th May 1880
Promoted To Glory 10th June 1957
They were united in love to God
and the Salvation Army'.
Mason: Winters c1929.

Abney House Corner   S/O6

46 Grave of General William Booth. The Salvationists' unique epitaphs are a microcosm of their robust faith. Upon the shield is inscribed in gilt letters – 'William Booth   Founder & 1st General Of The Salvation Army   Born 1829   Born Again Of The Spirit 1845   Founded The Salvation Army 1865   Went To Heaven 20th August 1912   Also Catherine Booth   The Mother Of The Salvation Army   Born 1829   Went To Heaven 4th October 1890'.
The triple headstone (left) commemorates First Commissioner George Scott Railton and other early leaders.

BOSTOCK, Frank Charles   1866-1912

Menagerist.

47   Life-size sleeping lion of white marble sprawled out on a high rectangular pedestal. Similar to the Wombwell monument at Highgate. Mason: Millward and Co Opposite Cemetery.

Road F   N/J5

BRAIDWOOD, James   1800-1861

Superintendent of the London Fire Engine Establishment 1832-61; AICE. Earlier Braidwood had organised the first efficient fire brigade in his native Edinburgh, just in time for a great conflagration which destroyed much of the High Street in 1824. On 22 June 1861 his life was claimed in the Tooley Street fire at Cotton's Wharf near Southwark, when a falling wall crushed and buried him. It took two days to recover his mutilated body. The funeral on 29 June was a public spectacle equal almost to the Tooley Street fire itself which raged on for a fortnight and caused damage estimated at about £2 million.
     Pedestal monument of white stone.

Branch B   W/N6

BRIGGS, George   1848-1925

Alderman and Sheriff of the City of London, JP and member of the Court of Common Council.

24   Elegant white marble monument in the form of a domed classical baldaquin, supported on four freestanding Roman Ionic columns. Mason: Millward and Co Sculptors, Opposite Cemetery c1925.

Entrance Drive   N/J11

BROCK, Rev Dr William   1807-1875

Baptist divine. First minister of Bloomsbury Chapel 1848-72, he started life as a watch-maker in Hertford.
     White marble headstone with lobed top.

Dr Watts' Walk   W Ranks/M6

47 Lion tomb of Frank Bostock

BURDER,   1783-1864
Rev Dr Henry Forster

Congregationalist divine. Minister at St Thomas Square Chapel, Hackney; Tutor in Philosophy and Mathematics at Hoxton Academy, afterwards at Highbury College.
     White stone chest tomb with hipped top. Mason: Cusworth c1859.

Dr Watts' Walk   W/M6

BUZACOTT, Rev Aaron   1829-1881

Congregationalist minister, and Secretary of the Anti-Slavery Society. He was the son of a South Seas missionary of the same name.
     Pedestal monument of stone. Mason: Dunkley of High Street, Stoke Newington c1877.

Yew Walk   S/L9

CAKEBREAD,   1833-1861
Harriett Elizabeth

Wife of William Cakebread of Bethnal Green.

48   Gothic monument of white marble with a tall square panelled pedestal supporting a richly crocketed pinnacle. Mason: Cusworth c1861.

New Road   N/J7

48 Harriett Cakebread's monument

CALVERT, Edward　　　　**1799-1883**

Painter and wood engraver. A disciple of William Blake, he was one of a group of English romantic artists who gathered around Samuel Palmer at Shoreham in the later 1820s and early '30s. Calvert's finest works are the exquisite miniature wood-engravings which date from this early period; much of his subsequent life was spent in obscurity at Dalston and Hackney. His wife Mary was the first to be interred here in 1869.

Self-effacingly plain headstone with curved top, the inscriptions now badly weathered, 1869. 'He was welcomed in Helicon'.

Mount Road　　E Ranks/C7

CAMPBELL, Rev Dr John　　　**1795-1867**

Congregationalist divine. Minister at Whitefield's Tabernacle and a stickler for orthodoxy. He founded and edited a number of Christian magazines and journals including the *Christian Witness* and the *British Banner*.

Pedestal monument.

Road E　　N/N6

CAULKER, Thomas Canry　　**1846-1859**

Young son of Canrah Bah Caulker, King of Bompey in Western Africa. Sent to England for a Christian education, he died at Canonbury while in the care of Rev Jacob Kirkman Foster.

Headstone unidentified.

Mount Road　　W/F7

CLARKE, Ebenezer　　　　**1797-1875**

Of Walthamstow. A Trustee and Director of the Abney Park Cemetery Company from 1866 until his death in 1875. Also commemorated is his son James, cruelly murdered in the State of Missouri in 1868.

White stone pedestal with draped urn, c1857.

Road G　　E/I5

CLAYTON, Rev John　　　　**1754-1843**

Independent divine. Pastor of The King's Weigh House Chapel in Eastcheap, City 1778-1826, and father of three Congregationalist ministers of repute. The elder Clayton and his third son, buried at first in Bunhill Fields, were transferred to Abney Park when the family tomb was brought here in 1857. Rev John Clayton (1780-1865) the eldest son, was pastor of Camomile Street Chapel 1805-19 then removed to the Poultry Chapel, City 1819-48. His younger brother Rev George Clayton (1783-1862) was pastor of York Street Chapel, Walworth 1804-54; and the third son Rev William Clayton (1785-1838), pastor at Saffron Walden 1809-31, later became chaplain to the Mill Hill Grammar School 1831-38.

Plain stone chest tomb with hipped top, brought from Bunhill Fields.

Dr Watts' Walk   E/M6

CONDER, Josiah   1789-1855

Bookseller, poet and author. The self-educated son of Thomas Conder, a City bookseller and map engraver, whose business he inherited in 1811. As a leading apologist for Congregationalism he was editor of *The Eclectic Review* 1814-37, and of *The Patriot* 1832-55; compiled the thirty volumes of *The Modern Traveller* 1825-29; author of numerous verses, essays, tracts etc including *The Poet of the Sanctuary, I. Watts* 1851, and *Hymns of Prayer and Praise* 1856. His wife Joan Elizabeth née Thomas (1785-1877), also interred here, was a grand-daughter of the sculptor Louis François Roubillac.

Chest tomb of grey polished granite with hipped top, 1856.

South Boundary Road A   N Ranks/M9

COOMBS, Thomas Merriman   1790-1863

Of Ludgate Street, City of London; later of Clapham Common. One of the Founders and first Trustees of the Abney Park Cemetery Company 1838-63, also Treasurer of New College at St John's Wood 1851-63.

Dark polished granite coffin tomb with hipped top. Mason: Piper of Norwood 1864.

Dr Watts' Walk   W/M6

CORFIELD, Joseph William   1809-1888

An admirer of nineteenth century social activists, he erected in Kensal Green Cemetery in 1885 an obelisk known as the Reformers' Memorial, 'to the memory of men and women who have generously given their time and means to improve the conditions and enlarge the happiness of all classes of society', upon which the names of fifty well-known reformers were inscribed. Another twenty-five were added in 1907 on the instructions of Corfield's daughter Emma.

The Corfield family grave dates from 1843.

Little Elm Walk   W Ranks/D6

CUSWORTH, John   1795-1856

Founder of John Cusworth and Sons, monumental masons, of High Street, Stoke Newington. The firm was established in 1819 and maintained branches at Pentonville Hill and in Scotland. Also buried here are John Cusworth junior (1825-1855) and his brother Thomas James Cusworth (died 1895).

Pedestal monument of grey granite. Mason: inevitably Cusworth, although not signed, c1856.

South Boundary Road A   N/M9

DELPH, Harriet   1862-1944

Of Clapton Square, Hackney.

A sophisticated small monument of white stone in the School of Arts and Crafts tradition; the stylised female mourner surmounts a cubic pedestal carried on a bold weathered podium by way of an abbreviated neck. Fine italic inscriptions in the manner of Edward Johnston, the designer of London Transport's lettering. Who might the sculptor have been? Mason: Winters of Stoke Newington 1946.

Path N   S/G3

DENNIS, William   1787-1866

Of Hackney. An early Director of the Abney Park Cemetery Company, he was appointed as one of the new Trustees in 1866 but died two months later. His eldest son William Thomas Dennis (1820-1899), also of Hackney, became a Trustee of the Company later in 1866 and was one of the four survivors of the old

40

49 Granite cross to Dr Alexander Fletcher, The Children's Friend

regime in 1882. He too is buried here.

Stone pedestal with diagonal inverted consoles at corners, surmounted by an urn on a wreathed base, c1852. **45c**

Dr Watts' Walk   S/M6

DUKES, 1809-1876
Rev Hezekiah Clement

A dissenting minister at Dalston.

Square stone monument with Tudor arched inscription panels, surmounted by a square finial from which rises a tall pyramidal spike and ball. Mason: Dunkley c1848.

Yew Walk   N/K7

DUNKLEY, Henry 1817-1900

Monumental stonemason and sculptor. Successor to the family business established in Hoxton 1835, but subsequently transferred to new premises adjoining the entrance to Abney Park Cemetery. Other branches were later opened at Cripplegate and Ilford.

The monument, of polished red granite, was erected for his wife Charlotte Elizabeth Dunkley (1820-1876) to supersede an earlier family memorial. Square pedestal supporting a plain broken column. Mason: Dunkley, High Street, Stoke Newington 1876.

Road I   S/I7

EDMOND, Rev Dr John 1815-1893

First minister of Highbury Presbyterian Church.

The grey granite obelisk monument has been toppled by bomb blast and re-erected.

Abney House Corner   N/O6

ELLERM, Amelia 1830-1855

Young wife of John Ellerm of Kingsland Road, London.

Delicately executed white marble monu- **27** ment consisting of a tall battered pedestal with deeply carved neo-Grec pediments, surmounted by a fluted broken column hung with a wreath. Mason: J S Farley of Goswell Road, Clerkenwell 1855.

Road I   S/I8

ELLIS, Rev William 1804-1872

Congregationalist missionary in the South Sea Islands and Madagascar; sometime Secretary of the London Missionary Society, and minister at Hoddesdon. He translated the Bible into Malagasy.

Low gothic chest tomb of pale terracotta with hipped topstone, long partially submerged beneath the huge debris of monuments destroyed by bomb blast in the 1940s.

Road E   S/N6

FERGUSON, Rev Robert 1806-1875

Congregationalist minister at St John's Wood. Founder and Secretary of the Pastor's Retiring Fund.

White marble coffin tomb with ridged top, to which was later added a small stone upright Latin cross.

Road I   S/I9

FLANDERS, William 1776-1854

Of Brunswick Square, Bloomsbury. Treasurer to the Society in the Connection of the Countess of Huntingdon, and a Director of the London Missionary Society.

White stone chest tomb with splayed sides and hipped top, 1854.

South Boundary Road A   W/M10

FLETCHER, 1787-1860
Rev Dr Alexander

Presbyterian divine – 'The Prince of Preachers to Children'. From 1810 pastor of Miles Lane Meeting House, afterwards moved to Albion Chapel in Moorfields. Displaced by his presbyters Fletcher founded the Finsbury Chapel in 1825 and continued his ministry there as an Independent.

Monumental high cross of polished red **49** granite with a pierced octagonal cross head of webbed outline; erected by his congregation. Mason: W H Burke and Co of Newman Street, Marylebone c1861.

Road E   N/N6

FLETCHER, Rev Dr Joseph   **1784-1843**

Independent minister of the Stepney Meeting House.

A massive obelisk monument of hammer-dressed grey granite; erected by his congregation. Mason: MacDonald of Aberdeen c1843.

Cedar Path   N/L8

FORSYTH, Agnes   **1861-1864**

'In Memory of Agnes, the Beloved Daughter of James and Eliza Forsyth, Died November 1, 1864, Aged Three Years and Eight Months' – so ran the inscription, now hopelessly weathered away. The girl's father was one of the most eminent architectural sculptors of his day, James Forsyth (1826-1910), whose best-remembered work is the great fountain of Perseus and Andromeda in the gardens of Witly Court, Worcestershire. His wife Eliza (1834-1867) is buried here too.

41 Agnes' exquisite monument, designed and executed by her father in the High Victorian gothic style, is in the form of a wayside shrine with steeply hipped scalloped roof and finial, white stone splayed onto a red sandstone base. Sculpture panels are recessed in a shafted arch front and back: firstly the delicate medallion portrait of Agnes, then on the reverse, a figure group representing Christ blessing little children. Mason/Sculptor: James Forsyth of Edward Street, Hampstead Road, St Pancras 1865.

South Boundary Road A   N/M10

FOSTER, Rev Jacob Kirkman   **1786-1861**

Minister in the Countess of Huntingdon's Connexion. Sometime President of Cheshunt College, at which he was a resident tutor for thirteen years.

Stone pedestal monument with curly pediment, the inscriptions practically illegible, 1861.

South Boundary Road A   S/N7

FOULGER, John   **1783-1850**

Of Walthamstow. A Founder-Trustee of the Abney Park Cemetery Company 1838-50.

Stone pedestal with cross-pediments. Mason: Millward of Stoke Newington 1850.

Road D   W/L6

GILBERT, Rev Charles   **1798-1878**

Congregationalist minister at Islington Chapel. Founder of Barnsbury Chapel, and Secretary of the London Chapel Building Society.

White headstone with ogee top, 1876.

Dr Watts' Walk   E Ranks/M6

**HABERSHON,
Catherine Sarah Caroline**   **1844-1848**

Young daughter of the architect William Gillbee Habershon (1818-1891) of St Neots, Huntingdonshire, where he had established practice in 1843. Son of Matthew Habershon (qv), he returned to London in 1849 and entered into partnership with his brother Edward at Bloomsbury. Catherine was originally buried at St Neots but in 1852 her remains were transferred to the plot next to her grandfather's in Abney Park.

50 The white gothic headstone with steeply gabled top, crockets and poppy-head finial, designed by W G Habershon for St Neots in 1848, was brought here with the reinterment.

South Boundary Road A   N/M10

50 The Habershon headstone (on right) among other gothic memorials in Road A

HABERSHON, Matthew   **1789-1852**

Architect, of St Marylebone, London. A devoted member of the Church of England, he published scriptural studies in the 1830s and '40s and was responsible for the completion of St James Cathedral in Jerusalem in 1842. Author of *The Ancient Half-Timbered Houses of England* 1836, a pioneer work in architectural history. His two sons, William Gillbee and Edward Habershon, were architects and probably designed his gothic headstone in 1852; the new Harecourt Congregational Church at Highbury 1855-56 was an example of their joint work.

The memorial no longer stands.

South Boundary Road A   N/M10

HALL, John Vine   **1774-1860**

A Maidstone bookseller and advocate for temperance. As a reformed alcoholic and convert to Christianity he wrote *The Sinner's Friend* 1821, which went through 356 editions and was translated into thirty languages. Retiring to Kentish Town in 1850, he became an elder at Surrey Chapel where his son was minister.

The original gravestone has been replaced by a more appropriate one to Dr Newman Hall (qv).

Road H   S/I3

HALL,   **1816-1902**
Rev Dr Christopher Newman

Congregationalist divine; son of John Vine Hall. Succeeded Rev James Sherman as minister of Surrey Chapel, Blackfriars in 1854. He was a friend of Gladstone, the high-church Prime Minister, and sought closer relations between the Established Church and dissent. Founder and first minister of Christ Church, Westminster Bridge Road 1876-92. Edited his father's autobiography *Conflict and Victory* 1865, then wrote his own *Newman Hall: An Autobiography* 1898.

Coffin tomb of polished red granite bearing a Latin cross recumbent, 1902.

Road H   S/I3

HALLEY, Rev Dr Robert   **1796-1876**

Congregationalist minister in Manchester, where he became known as a champion of working class liberation. Succeeded Dr John Harris as Principal of New College 1857-72.

Stone coffin tomb with hipped top, c1866.   **35**

Road G   E/L5

HARRIS, Rev Dr John   **1802-1856**

Congregationalist divine. A masterly preacher, he 'blazed like a meteor upon the religious world' with the publication of his *Mammon*. As a result he was appointed President of Cheshunt College in 1837, then Principal and Professor of Theology at New College in St John's Wood 1851-56.

Tall pedestal monument of grey granite surmounted by an urn, 1857.

Dr Watts' Walk   W/M6

HARRY, Rev Nun Morgan   **1800-1842**

Congregationalist minister at the City Chapel in Broad Street, London. Secretary to the Society for Promoting Permanent and Universal Peace.

Buried tomb slab.

Road E   N/N6

HART, Andrew   **1806-1868**

Of Stoke Newington.

Neoclassical white stone obelisk monument **51** forming a pair with that of his brother John Hart of Islington (1799-1871); this somewhat lugubrious group retains its ornamental cast iron rail surround, c1850.

Dr Watts' Walk   E/L6

HASTIE, Benjamin   **1786-1865**

Of Shacklewell Green.

His skeletonised gothic chest tomb, with **42** ridged topstone supported on three transverse uprights pierced with circular plate-tracery, was designed and executed by the sculptor James Forsyth in 1865.

Path D   S/M10

51 Twin obelisks of Andrew and John Hart

52 Identical headstones to William Hone and his sixth daughter Rose

HENDERSON, 1784-1858
Rev Dr Ebenezer

Congregationalist theologian. Agent of the British and Foreign Bible Society in Iceland, Scandinavia and Russia. Theological Tutor at Hoxton Academy and its successor institution, Highbury College.

Pedestal monument of grey granite, 1859.

Path B   E/L7

HIBBERD, James Shirley 1825-1890

Horticulturalist. Editor of *Floral World* 1858-75, and of *Gardener's Magazine* until 1890. A vegetarian and teetotaller, he experimented with fruit trees and vegetables, notably potatoes. Lived in Stoke Newington until the 1880s but kept removing further into the suburbs for the better pursuit of his gardening operations. Author of *Profitable Gardening* 1863 and *Familiar Garden Flowers* 1879.

The white gothic headstone, its gable decorously edged with foliage and carved with a small cross, was originally erected to his first wife Sarah Elizabeth in 1880. Inscriptions are seriously weathered.

South Boundary Road A   E/K10

HONE, William 1780-1842

Bookseller and author of *The Every Day Book*. A friend of Charles Lamb and a Deist, Hone was prosecuted for blasphemy in his satyrical *Political Litany* but acquitted after a historic three-day trial. Public subscriptions raised £3,000 for his costs. By the influence of Dr Thomas Binney of King's Weigh House Chapel, he subsequently converted to Christianity. Charles Dickens witnessed his funeral.

Plain neoclassical headstone with pedi- **52** ment, 1843.

Mount Road   W/H7

HOOD, Rev Edwin Paxton 1820-1885

Congregationalist minister at Falcon Square Chapel, London. Biographer of Oliver Cromwell, Isaac Watts, William Wordsworth and Dr Thomas Binney.

Tomb slab of polished red granite with stone rocks piled at its head, 1886.

Abney House Corner   S/N7

HUNT, John Alfred 1824-1913

Of Upper Clapton and Enfield. Son of William Hunt (qv), he was a Trustee of the Abney Park Cemetery Company from 1866 until its reconstitution in 1882.

White stone pedestal monument surmounted by a wreathed and draped urn. Mason: Dunkley 1850s.

Cedar Path   N/L8

HUNT, William 1796-1866

Of Mount Pleasant, Upper Clapton. Named as one of the new Trustees of the Abney Park Cemetery Company in 1866, he died before taking up his appointment.

Obelisk monument of polished red granite, 1857.

Road D   E/L7

JAMES, Rev Thomas 1789-1873

Congregationalist minister of Milton Street Chapel, Cripplegate and afterwards of the Woolwich Chapel. Secretary of Highbury College, and of the Irish Evangelical Society.

Latin cross of grey stone with marble boss of Christ's head at its centre, 1874.

Path E   N/K9

JAY, John   1805-1872

Building contractor and stonemason, of 65 London Wall, City of London. His name is inscribed on the foundation stone of Abney Park Cemetery Chapel 1840, as its builder under William Hosking's direction.

53   Rich baroque sarcophagus of stone with curved belly, mounted on four lion's paws, and elaborately carved in relief at each end. Mason: almost certainly John Jay himself, 1853-54.

Dr Watts' Walk   W/L6

JEFFERSON, Rev John   1796-1882

Congregationalist minister of Abney Chapel, Stoke Newington, from 1831. During his pastorate the chapel was rebuilt on a larger site opposite Abney Mansion 1837-38. He was appointed as the first dissenting chaplain to Abney Park Cemetery 1840, but retired some twenty-five years later in favour of Rev Thomas Barker. Succeeded Nun Morgan Harry as Secretary to the Society for Promoting Permanent and Universal Peace 1842-48.

The family grave of Jefferson and Geary dates from 1845.

Great Elm Walk   W Ranks/H5

JOHNSON, Sir Walter   1845-1912

Of Upper Clapton. An original member of the London County Council, and Mayor of Hackney in 1901-02.

54   White marble baroque angel on a tall polished granite pedestal. Mason: Winters c1911.

Dr Watts' Walk   E/K6

KEELING, Enoch Bassett   1837-1886

Architect, surveyor and speculator, of Dunwood House, Paradise Row, Stoke Newington (now part of Church Street opposite Clissold Park). Although son of a Sunderland Wesleyan minister, Keeling is

53 The baroque sarcophagus of John Jay

remembered on account of his series of extraordinary churches for London Anglican congregations in a wildly vigorous version of High Victorian gothic. Sadly all have either disappeared or have been seriously mutilated, but they belonged exclusively to that period when he also designed the Wesleyan Methodist Chapel in Richmond Road, Dalston 1864 (now also demolished). His practice crumbled after a professional storm involving his crazy gothic design of the Strand Music Hall 1863-64, and in spite of a few atypical commercial commissions at the end of his life he never fully recovered. The diagnosis suggests that he died of drink.

Tragically the gravestone, designed in c1883 for his wife, Mary Newby née Harrison (1841-1882), has long since vanished.

Path C   N Ranks/L9

KELLEY, Rev Joseph   1802-1875

Congregationalist missionary at George Town, Demerara, who worked successfully for the abolition of slavery and for the conversion of the Indian tribes of the Essequibo River.

Pedimented white stone pedestal, c1876.

Path E   N Ranks/K9

54 Monument to Sir Walter
Johnson

KING, Robert Scarborough 1859-1860

23 A gracefully entasised tall column of glistening white marble surmounted by an urn, c1861.

Entrance Drive S/J11

KITCHING, 1866-1930
Theodore Hopkins

Commissioner of the Salvation Army and Secretary to William Booth.
  Conventionalised Salvationist triptych headstone of blue Pennant sandstone, whose inscription reports Kitching 'Promoted To Higher Service [From Paris] February 10th 1930, Aged 63 Years.' Mason: Winters c1925.

Abney House Corner S/O6

LARKING, 1810-1884
Alfred Joseph

Of Whitechapel and Brighton. An early Director of the Abney Park Cemetery Company, appointed Trustee in 1866 until the conveyance of 1882. Interred in the tomb of his father William Larking (1778-1843), he is also commemorated at Abney House Corner on that of his brother George Frederick Larking (1819-1906). There are unaccountable errors in the dates given on both inscriptions.
  Pedimented stone pedestal monument, 1843.

Road D W/M6

LEIFCHILD, 1780-1862
Rev Dr John

Congregationalist divine. A St Albans cooper briefly attached to Methodism, Leifchild was persuaded by Thomas Wilson (qv) to enter the Congregational Academy at Hoxton. He ultimately became a preacher of great power at Craven Chapel in Regent Street, where no less than 1,500 conversions have been ascribed to his twenty-four year ministry.
  Grey granite ledger, 1862.

West Boundary Road B W/D2

LEWIS, Rev Thomas 1777-1852

Independent minister of the Union Chapel, Islington 1806-52.

White stone chest tomb in the mannerist style with closely set pairs of attenuated consoles framing the inscription panels, 1852.

Dr Watt's Walk E/L6

LEYBOURNE, George 1842-1884

Music Hall artiste alias 'Champagne Charlie', who lived and died at No 136 Englefield Road, Islington. His daughter Florence married in 1895 the comedian Albert Chevalier (1861-1923), who is also buried here.
  Headstone with gabled top.

New Road N Ranks/J8

LODDIGES, Conrad 1821-1865

Horticulturalist, of Hackney. Son and successor of George Loddiges (1786-1846), he inherited the Hackney nursery in 1850 but due to increasing atmospheric pollution he shortly closed it down and sold the remaining stock to the Crystal Palace Company, of which his brother-in-law, Edward William Cooke, was a Director. Married into the Bowes family of Homerton, Conrad is interred in their family vault.
  Stone chest tomb.

Dr Watts' Walk W/L6

LUNTLEY, Josiah John 1793-1858

Of The Triangle, Hackney. A Founding Trustee of the Abney Park Cemetery Company 1838-58. Members of the undertaker W Luntley's family are also buried here, as well as Rev Dr Brewer (1813-1875), the minister of Shacklewell Chapel.
  Pedestal monument of white stone, 1844.

South Boundary Road A N/M8

LYNCH, Rev Thomas Toke 1818-1871

Congregationalist divine, poet and hymnwriter. Minister at Mornington Church, Hampstead Road, London for twenty-two years.
  Gothic headstone, 1871.

Road H N/H3

55 Wooden deadboard of Joseph Douglass Mathews

56 Mannerist headstone of Lancelot James Mayer

MANNERING, Rev Edward 1801-1875

Congregationalist minister, for fifty years, of the successive chapels at Jewry Street, Holywell Mount and Bishopsgate in the City of London.

Obelisk of polished granite, 1875.

Road I   S/I9

MARTIN, Rev Samuel 1817-1878

Congregationalist divine. First minister of Westminster Chapel which was rebuilt on a larger scale during his pastorate; he retired in 1877. Dean Stanley of Westminster, who jocularly referred to Martin as his nonconformist curate, wished to have him interred in the Abbey but contented himself with conducting the burial service at Abney Park instead.

Monolithic monument formerly bearing metal tablets.

Yew Walk   N/K9

MASON, Rev John 1781-1864

Wesleyan minister, of Stamford Hill. A Secretary of the Wesleyan Methodist Missionary Society from 1824.

Square gothic monument of white stone

surmounted by a typical classical urn replete with drape and garland, 1854.

Dr Watts' Walk   E/L6

MATHER, Rev James 1775-1840

Congregationalist minister of the Upper Clapton Chapel. His interment, the first in Abney Park Cemetery, took place on Tuesday morning, 3 June 1840, after a service at Claremont Chapel conducted by Rev Thomas Blackburn, Dr John Leifchild officiating at the funeral. Also buried here is his son Rev Dr Robert Cotton Mather of Finchley (1808-1877), Congregationalist missionary at Mirzapore in India 1838-73. Author of several religious works, he translated the Bible into Hindustani.

White marble neo-Grec sarcophagus with splayed sides and shallow relief decoration, 1840.

Path L   N/F6

MATHEWS, Joseph Douglass 1838-1923

Architect and surveyor in the City of London. FRIBA. FSI. Deputy of Dowgate Ward. Son, and briefly partner, of H Mathews, a City surveyor since the 1820s.

Rare wooden deadboard with a slim **55** encircled cross at its head, all joints demonstrably pegged together in the Arts and Crafts fashion. Designed by Mathews in 1921.

West Boundary Road B   E/M5

MAYER, Lancelot James 1819-1849

Of Hoxton.

A superbly mannerist buff headstone **56** whose sides slope discreetly out from the base. At the top, delicate winged scrolls intrude into each side of a pedimental ground displaying the depressed ovoid relievo of a downward-pointing hand bursting through clouds against a 'glory' background. The finger is doubtless intended to direct attention towards the beautifully varied inscription letters below. However, in this subtle design nothing may be taken for granted. Small footstone too. Mason: Millward, opposite Cemetery 1850.

Path T   N/E4

MECHI, Fanny   **1799-1845**

Fanny née Frost was the first wife of John
Joseph Mechi of Stamford Hill (1802-1880), an
enterprising City merchant turned agricul-
turalist, of Bolognese extraction. Founder of
the Tiptree Hall Farm in Essex 1841, he
afterwards published various works recording his progress there. Nominated Lord
Mayor of London in 1866, he was obliged to
withdraw owing to the failure of his
investments and he eventually died in bank-
ruptcy.

57   Massive raised rectangular pedestal upon
which kneels a solemn female mourner, all of
porous marble so weathered that the inscription is now barely visible, c1845.

Road C   W/J7

MEDHURST,   **1796-1857**
Rev Dr Walter Henry

Congregationalist missionary in the Far East
from 1818 onwards, he established a mission
in Shanghai 1843, only returning to England a
few days before his death. Author of a
Chinese-English dictionary and translator of
the Bible into Mandarin.
   White stone obelisk monument, 1857.

Branch A   W/N6

MILLS, John Remington   **1798-1879**

Congregationalist benefactor, of Tunbridge
Wells. A nephew of Thomas Wilson (qv), Mills
was one of the wealthiest commoners in
England and already a millionaire before
inheriting his brother's considerable fortune.
   The severely plain stone chest tomb over the
family vault is an index of his thrifty Puritan
character; it is dated 1837 and was brought
here from Bunhill Fields in 1856.

Road D   W/M6

MORISON, Rev Dr John   **1791-1859**

Congregationalist minister at Trevor Chapel,
Brompton. Author of theological and bio-
graphical studies; editor of the *Evangelical
Magazine*.
   Pedimented pedestal of white marble, 1859.

Road E   N/N6

**57 Monument to Fanny
Mechi**

58 Chest tomb of James Bronterre O'Brien, a celebrated Chartist leader – 'His Life Was Grand His Death Was Sad and Drear' However, the inscription was mistaken as to his age.

59 Doomed schooner on the Orfeur cenotaph

Israel and *The Sword and The Harp.*

Headstone with curved and foliaged top, c1893.

Road I   S/I6

O'BRIEN,   1805-1864
James Bronterre

Political activist, journalist, and a prominent leader of the Chartist movement. Irish born, O'Brien graduated at Dublin University before completing law studies at Gray's Inn, London. During 1831 he became editor of a popular radical newspaper, the *Poor Man's Guardian*. An early advocate for land nationalisation, he was imprisoned for 18 months in 1840 for 'seditious speaking' at a meeting in Liverpool. In later life he lectured at the John Street Institute and at the Eclectic Institute in Soho, but apparently died in reduced circumstances. His influence was carried forward by his followers into the 1870s socialist revival.

White stone chest tomb with splayed sides **58** and moulded topstone, c1865.

Path B   E/L7

OFFOR, George   1787-1864

A prominent Congregationalist literary figure. Editor and biographer of John Bunyan.

Pedestal monument of red and grey polished granite. Mason: Cusworth 1864.

Road F   S/K6

ORFEUR, Henry Valentine   1799-1863

Of Great Yarmouth. The monument was first inscribed as a cenotaph to his two seafaring sons – 'Sacred to the memory of Henry Orfeur, lost, with all the crew, by the wreck of the schooner "Invoice", in the Bristol Channel, November 23rd, 1856, aged 23 years. Also John, his brother, of the barque "Geraldine", last heard of April 14th, 1862, near the equator, aged 27 years'.

A white stone and marble pedestal surmounted by a draped and wreathed urn. Heading the inscription panel, a small but **59** vivid sculptural relief represents the tempest tossed schooner in its final throes: 'The Sea

MORLEY, Samuel   1809-1886

MP for Nottingham and Bristol; a worker for nonconformist emancipation he endowed Morley College for adult education. His father, John Morley of South Hackney, was a notable Congregationalist. Also interred here is his brother John Morley of Upper Clapton (1807-1896).

Massy white stone chest tomb with a plain pediment to each end. Mason: Dunkley 1857.

Dr Watts' Walk   W/M6

NEWTON, Rev Dr Hibbert   c1817-1892

Preacher of the Gospel and, according to his confident epitaph, Epic Poet. His chief works were graced with such titles as *The Triumph of*

Shall Give Up Its Dead'. Mason: Cusworth 1863.

Road I   S/I8

OWEN, Sir Hugh   1804-1881

Methodist philanthropist and promoter of Welsh education; he was one of the originators of the University College of Wales at Aberystwith.

Modest family grave dating from 1867.

Path C   N/L10

PALMER, Rev William Stern   1787-1852

Congregationalist minister at Hare Court Chapel in Aldersgate.

Stone pedestal monument.

Statue Path B   S/K6

PERKS, Rev George Thomas   1820-1877

Secretary of the Wesleyan Foreign Missionary Society, and President of the Wesleyan Conference in 1873.

Obelisk monument of white marble 1877.

West Boundary Road B   W/M5

PHILIP, Rev Dr Robert   1791-1858   46

Congregationalist minister at Maberley Chapel in Balls Pond Road, Islington. Biographer of John Bunyan and George Whitefield.

Neoclassical grey granite headstone with plain pediment. Mason: A MacDonald of Aberdeen 1869.

Road E   N/N6

PYE SMITH, Rev Dr John   1774-1851

Congregationalist theologian and scholar. Author of *The Scripture Testimony to the Messiah* and a variety of other learned works; theological tutor of Homerton College 1805-50, and minister at the Old Gravel Pit Chapel in Chatham Place, Hackney 1811-50. Son of a Sheffield bookseller, Pye Smith was practically self-taught although he rose to be the first dissenting Fellow of the Royal Society and a Fellow of the Geological Society. Much to the consternation of his college governors, he also

joined ranks with a contentious group called the Anti-State-Church Society. His second son, Ebenezer Pye-Smith FRCS (1807-1885) is also buried here.

White stone and marble chest tomb surmounted by plain block-pediments. Mason: J S Farley 1851.

Dr Watts' Walk   E/L6

PYLE, Evelyn   1844-1893

Daughter of Conrad Loddiges of Hackney (1821-1865), and sister of the third Conrad Loddiges (died 1899) who was the last of the great horticultural family to be associated with Hackney. Evelyn married the Wesleyan minister Rev James Fawcett Pyle (1841-1913), who is also interred here together with six of their offspring.

Pink and grey polished granite pedestal surmounted by a draped urn. Mason: Cusworth 1893.

Abney House Corner   N/O6

RAILTON, George Scott   1849-1913

First Commissioner of the Salvation Army, 'Fell At His Post Cologne, July 19th 1913.' Typical Salvationist headstone of blue Pennant sandstone with gilt letters. Mason: Winters 1913.

Abney House Corner   N/O6

RALEIGH, Rev Dr Alexander   1817-1880

Congregationalist divine and an eminent preacher. Minister at Harecourt Chapel in Highbury; then founder of the new Congregational Church at Stamford Hill, built to the designs of John Tarring 1870-71 and sadly demolished 1965. His funeral was attended by the Vicar of Kensington, in which district he latterly served.

Tomb surmounted by a rough-hewn block of granite, 1881.

Abney House Corner   S/O7

REED, Rev Dr Andrew   1787-1862

Congregationalist philanthropist and hymnwriter. Son of a London watchmaker, but relinquished his family career to study theology under Rev George Collison at Hackney 1807. Minister at Cannon Street Road then at Wycliffe Chapel, Stepney for fifty years 1811-61, he was the founder of five important charitable institutions including the London Orphan Asylum at Clapton and the Royal Hospital for Incurables at Putney. His eldest son, Rev Andrew Reed of St Leonards on Sea (1817-1899), is also interred here.

Tall obelisk monument of polished red granite. Mason: Burchell of Hastings 1862.

Road E   S/N6

REED, Andrew Holmes   1848-1892

Second son of Sir Charles Reed MP (qv). Also buried here is his younger brother Talbot Baines Reed (1852-1893), author of books for boys, literary historian and Honorary Secretary to the Bibliographical Society of which he was a co-founder in 1892.

Monumental high Celtic cross encrusted **60** with splendid bold relief patterning; Celtic letters to inscriptions on base. Executed in Kilkenny of sparkling grey Irish granite. Mason: O'Shea, Kilkenny, Ireland 1893.

Abney House Corner   N/O6

REED, Sir Charles   1819-1881

Of Homerton and Tottenham. Second son of Dr Andrew Reed and an eminent lay Congregationalist. Printer, typefounder, educationalist and antiquary, Reed, as a Liberal, was elected the first MP for the Borough of Hackney 1868-74. Chairman of the School Board for London 1873-81, he was also a Trustee and Director of the Abney Park Cemetery Company 1866-81. Among those commemorated here is his eldest son, Rev Charles Edward Baines Reed (1845-1884), Secretary of the British and Foreign Bible Society, who met with an accidental death in the Engardine and was buried at Pontresina.

Obelisk monument of polished grey granite, 1881, felled by bomb blast but now re-erected.

Abney House Corner   N/N6

60 Celtic cross to Andrew Holmes Reed

61 Neoclassical headstone of Ann Rippen

REYNOLDS, Rev John   1782-1862

Congregationalist minister at Halstead. Son of a physician in the Court of King George III, Reynolds had distinguished himself as a classical scholar and civil servant before abandoning the Established Church for nonconformity under the guidance of Dr John Pye Smith. He was one of the earliest to be elected Chairman of the Congregational Union.

Plain pedestal monument, 1862.

Yew Walk   S Ranks/L8

RICHARD, Henry   1812-1888

Congregationalist minister of Marlborough Chapel, Old Kent Road, London 1835-50. As Secretary to the Society for Promoting Permanent and Universal Peace 1848-84 he relinquished the ministry to concentrate on the Society's anti-war campaigns, and was elected MP for Merthyr Tydfil 1868-88.

His imposing white stone and marble tomb **33** is in the form of an arcaded early English gothic shrine, with a stone ridge-roof steeply gabled at each end. Set in the front arch is a marble portrait medallion in high relief. Erected by public subscription 1891.

Abney House Corner   S/O6

RIPPEN, Ann   1810-1849

Wife of William Rippen.

A truly monumental headstone in severest **61** neoclassical style. The tall thick slab of grey pitted limestone rises at its top to a perfect semicircle, with concentrically applied white marble medallion above weatherbeaten inscriptions. The relief subject has a gracefully draped female mourner standing, head bowed, against a tomb shrouded by weeping willow, 1849.

Great Elm Walk   W/D5

ROBINSON, Samuel   1751-1833

Architect and surveyor, of Hackney. Founder of the Retreat Almshouses in Hackney 'for the comfort of twelve widows of protestant dissenting ministers, professing Calvinistic principles', built in the late gothic style 1812 from Robinson's designs. His other works include the nearby terrace called The Paragon 1810-13, and the Homerton Dissenters' College 1823. He and his wife Martha (1756-1836) were originally buried in the Retreat's forecourt, but when that building was demolished in 1901 they were reinterred in Abney Park.

The white stone gothic chest tomb with its **62** rich tracery panelling, designed by Robinson himself, was brought here with them and given a new top by Dunkley 1901.

Road I   S/I9

ROGERS, Dr Nathaniel   1808-1884

Doctor of medicine. Donor of stained glass memorial windows in St Paul's Cathedral, Westminster Abbey, City Temple and elsewhere.

'Dr. Rogers's Family-Tomb' proclaims an **32** inscription over the entrance to this, the one proper mausoleum of the entire cemetery. A white marble single-cell temple of the Corinthian order, with pedimented stone roof, c1864. It stands in a most eligible

62 Samuel Robinson's gothic chest tomb from the Retreat at Hackney

position once occupied by the front door to Abney House.

Abney House Corner   N/O6

SHARPE, Samuel   1799-1881

A banker and eminent Egyptologist. Author of *The History of Egypt* and translator of numerous Hebrew texts.

Plain stone chest tomb, 1881.

Dr Watts' Walk   E/M6

SHERMAN, Rev James   1796-1862

Congregationalist divine and popular preacher. Successor to his friend Rowland Hill as minister at the Surrey Chapel, Blackfriars 1836-54; latterly minister of Blackheath Congregational Church 1854-62. Author of *The Pastor's Wife* 1848, and other memoirs, he was one of the Founder-trustees of the Abney Park Cemetery Company 1838-62.

Plain stone chest tomb, 1848.

Road H   S/H3

SIEVEKING, Edward Henry   1790-1868

A merchant, linguist and leading municipal figure in Hamburg, also established in London from 1809. His wife Emerentia Louisa Francisca (1789-1861), the first interred here, was a daughter of Senator Meyer of Hamburg. They were the parents of Sir Edward Henry Sieveking MD.

Cruciform gothic coffin tomb, 1862.

Path T   N/E3

SIEVEKING,   1816-1904
Sir Edward Henry

Physician in ordinary to Queen Victoria 1888-1901; physician extraordinary to the Prince of Wales, afterwards King Edward VII 1873-1904. MD. FRCS. LLD. Knighted in 1886. Author of various medical works and an excellent watercolour illustrator of anatomical figures.

Gothic headstone with crocketed gable top, inscribed in gothic black letters, c1865. 'Now we see through a glass darkly but then face to face'. His wife Lady Jane Sieveking (1825-1915) is buried nearby to the east.

Path T   N/E3

SMITH, Rev Dr George   1803-1870

Congregationalist minister at Trinity Chapel, Poplar 1841-69; Secretary to the Congregational Union of England and Wales. Previously a home missionary in the ports of Bristol, Liverpool and Plymouth, Smith was appointed to the new dockland mission at Poplar by its founder George Green, a shipbuilder at Blackwall who had commissioned Hosking to design his chapel in 1840. A partner in the shipyard, William Wells, was at this time engaged in landscaping the grounds of his country house at Redleaf, Kent with the help of Edward William Cooke and other painter friends.

Plain pedestal monument of pink granite.

New Road   N/J7

SPENCE, Rev Dr James   1821-1876

Congregationalist divine. Minister at the Poultry Chapel, London 1854-67, then at the Old Gravel Pit Chapel in Hackney 1867-71. During his charge here the grand successor chapel at Clapton Park was erected 1869-71 to designs by Henry Fuller, but Spence was compelled through ill health to retire soon after its opening. Editor of *The Evangelical Magazine* until 1876. His brother, Rev Robert Spence (1823-1870), is buried close by.

Obelisk monument of polished grey granite. Mason: A Nicolson, Mark Lane, London 1876.

Catacomb Walk   S/J6

SPREAT, John   1799-1865

Of Highbury New Park, London. A prominent Congregationalist with business interests in Manchester; hence no doubt the choice of Alfred Waterhouse FRIBA (1830-1905), architect of the prestigious Manchester Assize Courts in 1859-64, as designer of his monument.

38   A severe essay in High Victorian gothic, chunky and four-square, in two diminishing stages surmounted by a now restored scalloped pyramidal cap; armorial bearings in relief on lower panel. All of brittle white limestone, 1866.

Chapel Lawn   N/G6

63 Epitaph to John Swan

SWAN, John   1787-1869

Engineer and inventor, of Kingsland, London. The pathos of his epitaph reveals Swan as a typical victim of nineteenth century class distinction. Credited by his daughter as the originator of such revolutionary devices as the steamship's screw propeller (1824) and the self acting chain messenger (1831), he never patented his inventions but allowed them to be published under the names of his superiors.

63   Stone pedestal surmounted by a draped and wreathed urn. Mason: Millward 1869.

Road I   N Ranks/H8

THORESBY,   1817-1883
Rev Thomas Elisha

Minister of the Countess of Huntingdon's Connexion at Spa Fields Chapel, Clerkenwell 1846-82. A leader of the Free Church of England.
        Grave covered in ivy and brambles at the time of writing.

New Road   N Ranks/J10

THORNTON,   1810-1865
Rev William Lockwood

A Wesleyan minister 'of singular wisdom and erudition'. President of the Wesleyan Conference 1865.
        Stone chest tomb in the gothic style with traceried panels, the inscriptions now barely legible, c1865.

North Boundary Road B   S/B6

TIDMAN, Rev Dr Arthur   1792-1868

Congregationalist missionary diplomat. Minister of the Barbican Chapel of the Old Protestant Dissenters' Set, in the City of London, and Secretary of the Irish Evangelical Society. He latterly served in the Foreign Secretariat of the London Missionary Society.

64   Small Veronese gothic baldaquin of white stone, enclosed with marble inscription panels and surmounted by a crocketed pyramidal spire, c1870.

Path A   N Ranks/L7

TOLLADY, Elizabeth   1827-1855

Wife of William John Tollady of Dalston.

65   Definitely the best piece of funerary angel sculpture in Abney Park Cemetery, not at all sentimental but with some of the awkward solemnity of prerafaelite paintings. Of white marble on a high pedestal with richly carved neo-Grec pediments. Mason: Dunkley 1855.

Chapel Lawn   E/H6

TYLER, William Frederick   1877-1909

Police Constable, murdered during an attempted arrest at Tottenham on 23 January 1909.

66   Stone and marble baldaquin monument in the Edwardian baroque style sheltering a well-sculptured police helmet and cape. Erected by the Metropolitan Police Force 1909.

Statue Path B   N/K6

VINCENT, Henry   1813-1878

Political agitator; known as the Demosthenes of the Chartist movement, of which he was a

64 Verona style monument to Dr Arthur Tidman

65 Elizabeth Tollady's prerafaelite angel

66 Edwardian baroque monument to PC William Tyler

leader. His wrongful imprisonment in 1839 sparked off fierce rioting. After release he made several attempts to enter Parliament, but although unsuccessful in their main objective his election campaigns propelled Vincent into his life's work as a popular orator on social, political and Christian issues.

Plain white headstone with semicircular top, 1850.

Path T   S/E4

WADE, David John   1857-1882

A young sculptor whose work so far remains obscure.

His grey granite grave-stele is an original **68a** conception made up of elemental gothic shapes but producing a total effect far removed from any medieval style. The pedimental top section displays a sensitive medallion portrait in low relief, encircled by attributions of industry, talent, modesty and truth, 1883.

Road I   N Ranks/I9

WALKER, Robert   1838-1896

Architect and surveyor, of Canonbury. FRIBA. FSI. District Surveyor for the parishes of St Martin in the Fields and St Anne Soho; a designer mainly of commercial buildings in London.

White stone pedestal monument. Mason: Gusworth 1884.

Road I   N/H7

WALKER, Sarah   1798-1847

Wife of Thomas Walker.

Four-square stone monument in lush **26** Puginian gothic, supporting a boldly crocketed spire with four small gables at its base. The arched inscription panels are elaborately cusped and decorated with carving in their spandrels, 1847.

Road I   S/I8

WATSON, Rev John   1804-1859

Congregationalist divine. Co-pastor with Thomas Lewis at the Union Chapel in Islington, and subsequently pastor of the chapel at Finchley. Succeeded Rev George Collison as President and theological tutor of Hackney College 1847-59. Watson was struck down by a cab on London Bridge and died from his injuries in St Thomas' Hospital.

Monument unidentified.

Dr Watts' Walk   E Ranks/L6

WATTS, Rev Dr Isaac   1674-1748

Independent divine, poet, hymnwriter and moral philosopher. Pastor at the Bury Street Chapel, City of London, from 1708 onwards. He died at Abney Mansion on 25 November 1748 after residing here for nearly fifteen years, and was interred at Bunhill Fields where his stone chest tomb (1749, renewed 1808) may still be seen.

The monument in Abney Park was erected **1** by public subscriptions in September 1845 and has a large statue by Edward Hodges Baily surmounting a high battered pedestal. It has recently undergone restoration and cleaning (1982) as a result of extensive but mysterious damage to the figure. The inscription is not to

67 Neoclassical obelisk to
Rev Algernon Wells

be relied upon in some of its more factual statements. Mason: Cusworth (for pedestal).

Dr Watts' Walk   Centre/K6

WELLS, Rev Algernon   1793-1850

Congregationalist divine. Pastor at Coggeshall 1818-37, then at Clapton Chapel 1839-50; joint Secretary of the Congregational Union and the Colonial Missionary Society 1837-50.

Massive broad granite obelisk of elemental **67** proportions, rising to a saddleback top instead of a conventional pyramid point, 1851.

Dr Watts' Walk   W/K6

WHYTE, Rev Thomas   1825-1860

First minister of the English Presbyterian Church at Dalston.

Grey granite pedestal monument, 1860.

West Boundary Road B   W/I3

WICKHAM, William   1782-1860

Social reformer, of Kingsland, London. A member of the several Boards of the Parish of Hackney, Wickham campaigned for parliamentary reform, free trade and freedom of election.

His pink granite obelisk monument was erected by the Hackney Parochial Reform Association. Mason: Cusworth 1860.

Chapel Lawn   N/G6

WILLIAMS, Rev John De Kewer   1817-1895

Independent minister. His epitaph proudly records the presentation of his portrait by the Lord Chief Justice Russell, to the Old Town Hall of Hackney, his native parish, in 1894.

White stone pedestal monument.

Statue Path B   S/K5

WILSON, Thomas   1764-1843

Congregationalist benefactor who derived great wealth from the manufacture of ribbon and from Remington family legacies; John Remington Mills was his nephew. Treasurer of Hoxton Academy and its successor Highbury College 1794-1843; a founder member of Council of University College, London from 1825; one of the founders of the Metropolis Chapel Fund Association in 1837, and an early Director of the London Missionary Society. Wilson built at his own expense several new Congregational chapels in London and elsewhere, the most famous being Claremont Chapel at Pentonville 1819, and Craven Chapel in Regent Street 1822. Also interred here is Rev James Stratton (1795-1872), for forty-two years minister at Paddington Chapel, another of Wilson's foundations, where the fashionable congregation included Robert and Elizabeth Barrett Browning.

Severely plain stone chest tomb, 1843.

Yew Walk   S/L7

WILSON, Thomas   1822-1876

Congregationalist schoolmaster; son of a deacon of the chapel at Hoxton, and founder of Southgate Road Middle-Class School in De Beauvoir Town, where he was headmaster for twenty-four years.

His slim obelisk monument of pink-grey polished granite was erected by some of his old scholars. Mason: Millward and Co c1876.

Branch D   E Ranks/G6

YOCKNEY, Rev John   1790-1852

Congregationalist minister at the Lower Street Meeting House, Islington 1815-45.

His chest tomb of polished red granite with long diagonal corner consoles displays mannerism in its fundamentalist variety, 1852.

Dr Watts' Walk   E/L6

YOUNG, Rev Dr John   1805-1881

Presbyterian divine and author of several abstruse religious studies. He was at one time pastor of the Albion Chapel, London Wall, Moorgate but resigned early from the ministry for theological reasons.

Grey granite headstone with semicircular top, 1881.

South Boundary Road A   N/M8

a

b

68 A group of four headstones

a David John Wade in Road I

b Agnes Susan Pesman in Path G

c Emma Elizabeth Wildish in Road H

d John Johnson in Road I

c

d

Nature in Abney Park Cemetery
the woodland in inner London
by Dr Alan Hunt

Abney Park provides many of the features of the typical rural woodland; for this reason it is of immense value and importance in such a densely populated borough as Hackney. It provides a habitat for wildlife that is normally only available many miles outside London; it thus brings an interesting section of the countryside to the people of the district. It has considerable potential too as a nature resource to the schools of the area.

The trees of Abney Park

The trees provide an interesting mixture of types and ages. Many of the trees remain from the carefully planned tree planting of the later Victorian period. The general planting scheme made use of Black Poplar, Lombardy Poplar in the east section nearest the main gates, Silver Birch in the south near Church Street and Horse Chestnut, Oak and again Poplars in the north section. The many ancient Elms in the north all succumbed to Dutch Elm disease and have recently fallen or been felled. Alongside these more common species there remain from the earlier planting some uncommon species which include Swamp Cypress, Indian Bean Tree, Service Tree of Fontainebleu, a variety of Pines and less common Oaks, such as Turkey Oak.

More recently there has been an invasion of fast growing Sycamore and Common Ash. There is an urgent need to control the number of these species which will otherwise engulf the existing varied vegetation and result in a vastly less interesting and diverse habitat.

The shrub layer is often dense. Brambles are prolific and widespread and produce excellent blackberries. Elderberry and various Hawthorns provide cover and a plentiful crop of berries for the birds. Ivy grows over many of the monuments and up the trunks of trees providing protection for insects and nest sites for birds. The death of the old Elms gave the tall and rapidly colonising Japanese Knotweed a niche in which to grow; it is currently spreading rapidly and is much in need of control.

The ground layer is restricted by the dense tree and shrub cover, as well as by the monuments and gravestones, but even so plenty of flowers appear during spring and summer. There is a mixture of species associated with woodland (Red Campion, Hogweed, etc) and with waste ground (Cow Parsley, Nipplewort, Sow Thistle, etc). Variety is added by many garden flowers growing wild (eg Michaelmas Daisy).

The birds of Abney Park

In spring and early summer the rich variety of bird song adds to the idyllic woodland aura of the cemetery, rendering the noise of the busy main roads more remote.

The bird life has been studied closely for the last few years and interesting results have been obtained. The cemetery is the most important site in Hackney and its neighbouring boroughs for woodland birds. It has a much greater diversity and density than that of the normal urban park.

Abney Park contains very large populations throughout its length and breadth of the common woodland and garden species (Blackbird, Song Thrush, Dunnock, Wren and Robin). The varied areas and habitats within the cemetery also attract different groups of birds. The shrubs and leafy glades attract warblers; Willow Warblers, Blackcaps, Chiffchaff, Spotted Flycatchers and occasionally Whitethroats return each spring from Southern Europe and Africa.

The dense tree canopy provides nesting sites for Mistle Thrush, Stock Dove, Woodpigeon, Jay, Magpie and Carrion Crow, while old mature trunks provide sites for hole-nesting species. Blue Tits and Great Tits are abundant; Coal Tits have bred and Starlings inhabit almost every Poplar tree. The presence of the Great Spotted Woodpecker is a truly woodland feature and the regular attendance of hooting Tawny Owls lends an aptly eerie quality to the cemetery's nocturnal aspect. The finches are represented by Greenfinch, Goldfinch and the striking but shy Bullfinch.

In summer large numbers of Swifts and House Martins and, less frequently, Swallows hunt insects overhead and around the spire of the chapel. Kestrel also hunt for prey in and around the cemetery.

Abney Park is also exploited by Mallards, probably from the water at Clissold Park. They nest in the dense undergrowth and are then faced with the massive task of guiding their downy chicks over the cemetery wall across Bouverie Road, through gardens and alleys across Lordship Road to Clissold Park. Few of the young Mallard can survive such a hazardous journey. Occasionally they get assistance from park-keepers who have been called upon by residents to rescue families from back gardens. Yet the adults return to breed in increasing numbers.

The cemetery also provides an important feeding area in winter, because being in such a built-up area it is warmer than the countryside outside London. In winter the resident birds are joined by Chaffinch, Linnet and Redpoll; the harder the weather the more important is the protected cemetery. In the hard winter of 1978-79 the uncommon Woodcock was recorded.

Other animal life

Other forms of animal life have not been studied as yet in any detail. However, cursory examination suggests the presence of an extensive insect population for whom the fallen leaves and timber are important. A good number of beetles are in evidence and the smaller moths are plentiful.

There is considerable room for more detailed study of the possible mammals and of all areas of insect life. There is, for example, much scope for projects to be undertaken by local schools. In general, the natural life here offers much of interest for local residents without their having to travel out to the country. Abney Park Cemetery brings an important slice of nature into the heart of London.

Sources and Further Reading

APC Office   Abney Park Cemetery Office, South Lodge, Stoke Newington High Street, N16

Guildhall   Corporation of the City of London Records, Guildhall Library, London EC2

LBH Archives   London Borough of Hackney Archives, Rose Lipman Library, De Beauvoir Road, N1

LBH Legal   London Borough of Hackney Legal Division, Town Hall, Mare Street, E8

SN LHC   Stoke Newington Local History Collection, Reference Library, Church Street, N16

The Abney Park Cemetery Company   Land Conveyance Documents, 1839-1979 [LBH Legal, Title Deeds File H4976].

The Abney Park Cemetery Company   Registers of Burials, 1840 onwards [APC Office. LBH Archives, duplicates].

The Abney Park Cemetery Company   Plot Plans, 1840 onwards [APC Office].

The Abney Park Cemetery Company   Catalogue of the Auction of Materials at Abney Park Mansion, Wednesday 26 July 1843 [LBH Archives].

The Abney Park Cemetery Company Limited   Land Companies' Reports, 1881 onwards [Stock Exchange Registrations, Guildhall].

Allerton, Richard   Map Of The Parish Of St. Mary Stoke Newington. 1848 [MS Tithe Survey with Index. SN LHC].

Barker, Thomas B   Abney Park Cemetery: A Complete Descriptive Guide To Every Part Of This Beautiful Depository Of The Dead. London 1869.

Beck, William   A Description of Church Street, Stoke Newington. London 1927. Compiled from notes made in 1890 by William Beck, Architect.

Boase, Frederic   Modern English Biography, 1851-1900. London 1965.

Burder, George (ed)   The Works of the Reverend and Learned Isaac Watts, D.D. six volumes. London 1810.

Collison, George — Cemetery Interment: Containing A Concise History Of The Modes Of Interment Practised By The Ancients; Descriptions of Père La Chaise, The Eastern Cemeteries, And Those Of America; The English Metropolitan And Provincial Cemeteries, And More Particularly Of The Abney Park Cemetery, At Stoke Newington, With A Descriptive Catalogue Of Its Plants And Arboretum. London 1840.

Colvin, Howard M — A Biographical Dictionary Of British Architects 1600-1840. London 1978.

Curl, James Stevens — A Celebration Of Death. London 1980.

Curl, James Stevens — The Victorian Celebration Of Death. Newton Abbot 1972.

The Dictionary of National Biography

Forsyth, James — A Book of Designs for Mural and Other Monuments. Third Edition. London 1867.

Fraser, Alan R — Abney Park Cemetery Ecology and management. Report to Hackney Borough Council Oct. 1979 [LBH Leisure Services].

French, James Branwhite — Walks In Abney Park With Life-Photographs of Ministers and other Public Men whose names are found there. London 1883.

Hall, Mrs S C — Pilgrimages to English Shrines: The Residence of Dr. Isaac Watts. Article with illustrations by F W Fairholt FSA, in Art Union Monthly Journal, 1848 pp 153-7.

Holmes, Mrs Basil — The London Burial Grounds. Notes on their History from the Earliest Times to the Present Day. London 1896.

Hood, Edwin Paxton — Isaac Watts; His Life and Writings, His Homes and Friends. London 1875.

Jones, R Tudur — Congregationalism in England 1662-1962. London 1962.

The Literary World, 30 May 1840 — Abney Park Cemetery. Article with a wood-engraving.

Loddiges — Manuscript notes on the Loddiges family. nd. [Hackney LHC, Central Reference Library, Mare Street, E8]

Loudon, John Claudius — On The Laying Out, Planting, And Managing Of Cemeteries. London 1843.

The Manor of Stoke Newington	Court Rolls, 1675-1882 [SN LHC, Transcriptions from originals in Guildhall].
Meller, Hugh	London Cemeteries An Illustrated Guide and Gazetteer. Amersham 1981.
Milner, Thomas	The Life, Times and Correspondence of the Rev. Isaac Watts, D.D. London 1834.
Robinson, William	The History And Antiquities Of The Parish Of Hackney. two volumes. London 1842-43.
Robinson, William	The History And Antiquities Of The Parish Of Stoke Newington. London 1820, reprinted 1842.
Shirren, A J	The Chronicles of Fleetwood House. London 1951.
Slinn, Judy	A History of Freshfields. London 1984.
Wright, Thomas	Isaac Watts And Contemporary Hymn-Writers. Volume III of The Lives of the British Hymn-Writers. London 1914.

69 Headstone of Joseph John Newman

Glossary

ACROTERIA — Carved blocks at the ends or top of a classical pediment, usually decorated with acanthus foliage.

APSIDAL — Semicircular or polygonal ended, as applied to church plans.

BALDAQUIN — Canopy supported on columns, generally over an altar or tomb.

BAROQUE — Dramatic three-dimensional version of the classical renaissance, emanating from early-seventeenth century Italy.

BATTER — An inclined upright plane or wall surface (cf Entasis).

CAMPO SANTO — Celebrated medieval cemetery in Pisa, built in quadrilateral form and enclosed by cloisters.

CAPITAL — Top part or head of a column.

CARTOUCHE — Inscribed tablet enclosed by an ornate frame.

CATACOMB — Subterranean gallery with side recesses for coffins.

CELTIC CROSS — Monumental high cross with encircled head and carved surface decoration; a type based on early medieval Irish examples. The circle is a symbol of eternity.

CENOTAPH — Sepulchral monument commemorating one who is buried elsewhere.

CHEST TOMB — Stone tomb in the form of a large rectangular chest.

CLERESTORY — Windowed upper storey of a church nave or hall.

COFFIN TOMB — Low horizontal tomb resembling a coffin.

CONSOLE — Curved or scrolled bracket; the inverted console is used as an ornament in mannerist and baroque architecture.

COPYHOLD — An obsolete form of land tenure resting on the custom of a manor and usually taken for the lifetime of the tenant and his immediate heirs; its renewal depended upon the discretion of the Lord of the Manor.

CROCKET — Projecting hook of carved foliage in gothic architecture, placed in series along the angles of a gable, pinnacle or spire.

CROSS DISC — A regular cross inscribed or carved in relief on a solid disc-shaped background.

CRUCIFORM — In the shape of a cross.

CUPOLA — A small dome, usually crowning a turret or lantern.

CUSP — Sharp point between the foils, or petal shapes, used as decoration in some gothic arches, especially in tracery or panelling.

DEADBOARD	Simple wooden board for inscriptions, held up between two posts.
DEMESNE	That part of domain, manor or estate retained in the owner's hands.
ENTASIS	Slight convex deviation from the straight line in a column etc, used to combat optical errors. Often taken as an alternative term for Batter (qv).
EPISCOPAL	Governed by bishops, as in the Established Church of England.
EPITAPH	An inscription on a tomb.
FINIAL	Crowning ornament of a gable, pinnacle, roof or spire, etc.
FLUTED	Vertically grooved or faceted, as applied to column shafts.
FOLIATED	Carved with conventionalised leaf shapes or foliage.
FOOTSTONE	Small upright slab at the foot of a grave.
FUNERARY URN	An empty carved urn symbolising death, derived from the antique classical cinerary urn. It may be wreathed, garlanded, draped or plain.
GOTHIC	Medieval European system of architecture dependent on the pointed arch, a style first brought to fulfilment in Northern France during the twelfth and thirteenth centuries. High Victorian gothic revivalists in mid-nineteenth century England admired the structural logic of this early French work and absorbed its boldest ideas into their own creative thinking (cf Puginian).
HEADSTONE	Upright stone slab for inscriptions placed at the head of a grave.
HOUSE TOMB	Large tomb with an architectural facade entered through a doorway.
KERB	Low stone rail surrounding a grave plot.
LANTERN	A roof-turret which is glazed all round.
LATIN CROSS	Plain cross with an elongated stem; in distinction from the Greek Cross which has all four arms equal in length.
LEDGER STONE	Horizontal tomb slab with inscriptions.
LUNETTE	Semicircular or similarly shaped panel or opening.
MANNERIST	Individualistic development of classical renaissance originating in early-sixteenth century Italy; a precursor style of the baroque (qv).
MAUSOLEUM	Tomb on an architectural scale which also serves as a monument.

NECROPOLIS	City of the dead; a cemetery.
NEOCLASSICAL	Purist revival of antique Greek and Roman art during the late-eighteenth and early-nineteenth centuries.
NEO-GEORGIAN	English Georgian revival in the early-twentieth century.
NEO-GREC	Revival of ancient Grecian forms in the late-eighteenth and early-nineteenth centuries.
OBELISK	Free-standing tapering pillar with blunt pyramidal point, usually of square section; antique Egyptian symbol of eternal life.
OGEE	Compound pointed arch with incurving lines towards its top.
OVERTHROW	Ornamental wrought iron arch or lintel over a gateway.
PALISADE	Close fencing or railing.
PALLADIAN	Restrained classical manner of eighteenth century English architecture, introduced in reaction against the baroque.
PEDESTAL MONUMENT	Upright construction like a pedestal, for the display of inscription panels, often surmounted by an urn.
PEDIMENT	Low pitched classical roof-gable, usually triangular but also with curved, broken or scrolled top and often used as an independent decorative feature.
PINDARIC ELEGY	Poem of lamentation for the dead, formalised by rules of the Greek poet Pindar.
PINNACLE	Ornamental crowning feature like a miniature spire.
PORTE COCHERE	Large open porchway for the reception of carriages.
PREBENDARY	Canon or member of a cathedral chapter whose stipend or salary was provided by his holding particular land forming part of the cathedral possessions.
PUGINIAN	Early version of the Victorian gothic revival following the more purely decorative manner of the architect Augustus Welby Northmore Pugin (1812-1852), and keeping faith with English medieval forms.
PYLONS	Tall structures flanking a gateway, especially in Egyptian architecture.
RELIEF	A piece of carving or sculpture in which the design stands out from its background surface; otherwise termed Relievo.
REREDOS	Ornamental panelling, screen or wall above the back of an altar; altarpiece.

ROCOCO	Fantastical late phase of baroque prevalent throughout much of Europe during the eighteenth century.
ROMANESQUE	Early medieval round-arched style dependent on ancient Roman systems; otherwise called Norman.
SARCOPHAGUS	Elaborately carved stone coffin, or a tomb resembling this.
SEPULCHRE	A tomb.
SKELETONISED	Reduced to basic structure and pierced.
SPANDREL	Bounded surface outside the curve of an arch, or the quasi-triangular space between two arches.
STELE	An upright grave slab of ancient classical origin, displaying inscriptions, symbols or sculptural representations.
TABLE TOMB	Horizontal tomb slab supported on legs or feet.
TRACERY	Intersecting ribwork in the upper part of a gothic window or decorative blank arch, etc. Plate-tracery is an early form where the openings are cut directly through solid stone infilling.
TRANSEPTS	The subsidiary crossing arms of a cruciform building.
TRIPTYCH	Three panels hinged together, usually to form a pictorial altarpiece.
VALHALLA	Burial place or collected monuments of a nation's illustrious dead.
VERMICULATION	Pitted surface texture achieved by numerous worm-shaped gouges.
VIGNETTE	A sketchy illustration with indefinite border, or with background shaded off.

Index

70 Plan of Abney Park Cemetery. The grid system follows the official plot plans kept at the cemetery office, and the names of the roads, walks and paths are those used in Thomas Barker's guide of 1869, with variants from a later cemetery plan. Prefixes N S E and W attached to the grid references in the text indicate on which side of a route each monument lies.

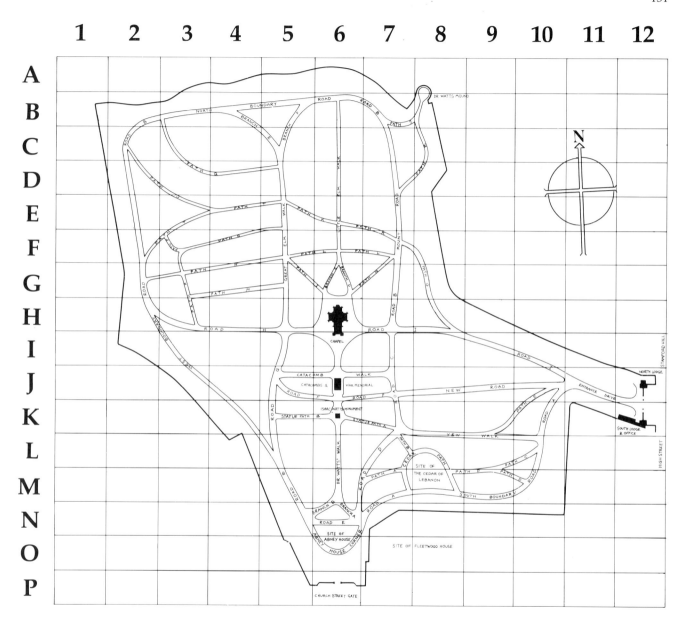

Text and Captions by Paul Joyce:
copyright © 1983, 1993 Paul R Joyce

Nature in Abney Park Cemetery
by Dr Alan Hunt: copyright © 1983 Alan Hunt

Illustrations Maps and Prints:
front cover and nos 8, 14 Author's Collection
no 3 The Salvation Army Archives
nos 4, 5, 6, 7, 10, 12, 13, 15, 20, 21 LBH Archives
no 11 LBH Legal Division

Drawings: nos 16, 17, 18 From the SAPC
Survey by Paul Joyce

Photographs: nos 1, 2, 9, 19, 22, 23, 24, 25, 26,
27, 28, 29, 30, 32, 33, 34, 35, 36, 37, 38, 40, 41,
45abc and d, 46, 47, 48, 49, 50, 51, 53, 54, 55, 56,
57, 60, 61, 64, 65, 66, 68ac and d, 69, and back
cover   Taken for the SAPC Survey of
Monuments by Paul Joyce:
copyright © 1983 Paul R Joyce
nos 31, 39, 42, 43, 44, 52, 59, 62, 63, 67, 68b
Taken for the SAPC Survey of Monuments by
Alan Tucker: copyright © 1983 Alan Tucker
no 58 Ian Priddey (Hackney People's Press):
copyright © 1983 Ian Priddey

Plan: no 70 Ian Wallace

Designed by Peter Gladwin
Printed by Expression Printers Ltd, London N5 1JT
ISBN 0 9509420 2 2